1975

ay be kept

IMPRISONED IN AMERICA
*Prison communications
1776 to Attica*

In The Supreme Court of The United States
Washington D.C.

Clarence Earl Gideon
            Petitioner
    vs.
H.G. Cochran,Jr, as
Director, Divisions
Corrections State
of Florida

Petition for a Writ
of Certiorari Directed
To The Supreme Court
State of Florida.

No. 890 Misc.

OCT. TERM 1961

U.S. Supreme Court

To: The Honorable Earl Warren, Chief
    Justice of the United States
        Comes now The petitioner, Clarence
Earl Gideon, a citizen of The United States
of America, in proper person, and appearing
as his own counsel. Who petitions this
Honorable Court for a Writ of Certiorari
directed to The Supreme Court of The State
of Florida. To review the order and Judgement of the court below denying The
petitioner a writ of Habeus Corpus.
        Petitioner submits That The Supreme
Court of The United States has The authority
and jurisdiction to review The final Judgement of The Supreme Court of The State
of Florida the highest court of The State
Under sec. 344(B) Title 28 U.S.C.A. and
Because The "Due process clause" of the

First page of Clarence Earl Gideon's communication
to the United States Supreme Court

IMPRISONED IN AMERICA

Prison Communications
1776 to Attica

edited by
CYNTHIA OWEN PHILIP

HARPER & ROW, PUBLISHERS
New York, Evanston, San Francisco, London

The editor wishes to acknowledge permission to reprint:

Ohio Penitentiary first-day cover. Thomas Licavoli.
Photograph by Robert Neese. Globe Photos, Inc.
Cartoons by Wade Eaves. State of Arkansas, Department of Correction.
Painting by Vernell Mitchell. Herbert Hemphill.
Photograph of D yard, Attica Correctional Facility, New York. Released by New York
    State Special Commission on Attica.

I should like to express my gratitude for the resources and the helpful staffs of The
Historical Society of Pennsylvania, The New-York Historical Society, the Union
Theological Seminary Library, and The New York Public Library; this anthology could
not have been compiled without them. I should also like to thank Marie Cantlon for
her valuable insights, C. Richard Anderson for copying the music of the Bradley
brothers' "Thanksgiving Song," and countless friends for suggestions and
encouragement. And I thank my family especially for their rare balance of interest,
humor, and endurance. Errors and oversights are entirely my own.

*To the prisoners whose communications
are presented in this anthology, and
to all prisoners*

INTRODUCTION

Of all the symbols of imprisonment, the massive wall is perhaps
the most expressive. For society has traditionally adopted an out
of sight, out of mind attitude toward those who offend; it has
believed that its security, prosperity, happiness, its very freedom
were dependent upon absolute protection from convicted
wrongdoers.

Not content with mere physical isolation, free society has
wholeheartedly supported the erection of extensive barriers to
inmate communication. Depriving criminals of the
Constitution's guarantee of free speech, it has condoned
unchallenged censorship by prison authorities of incoming and
out going written matter.

It was only in the 1960s that cases involving inmates' rights
to send uncensored letters and papers to courts were tried and
decided in favor of unrestricted communication; even today this
right is not protected in all jurisdictions. Correspondence
between inmates and attorneys is less free, some courts allowing
deletion of all material not specifically related to the legality of
the inmate's detention and treatment. Censorship of personal
mail is still accepted by courts, who are loath to look carefully at
what actually happens in prisons; they find censorship
appropriate to the criminal justice system's goals of
rehabilitation, retribution, deterrence, and restraint. To prison
administrators, inmate communication with the outside is a
privilege, not a right, and is therefore subject to whatever
controls they see fit to apply.

Not only is content scrutinized, but through approved

correspondence lists, the persons with whom a prisoner may correspond are screened; often only proven immediate family and attorneys are permitted. Frequency and length of letters are also controlled. Administrators have, in addition, extended censorship by withholding writing supplies such as paper, pencils, pens, ink, and typewriters; inmates usually must pay for them, as well as for postage, which operates in practice as a deterrent to many who have only the little money they can earn in prison, if indeed they are given that opportunity.

Manuscripts come under the same, if not stricter, bans as letters, and in 1971 prison officials endeavored to use a diary entry describing a guard in derogatory terms to incriminate an inmate for intramural punishment.

Incoming books, magazines and newspapers, radio and television, are also monitored, usually according to the taste and intellectual capabilities of the presiding official. For instance, among the publications recently proscribed in New York State were *The Jefferson Bible, The Blackstone Law Course, The Savage Mind*, a difficult work on the structural analysis of myth by Claude Levi-Strauss, and various issues of *National Geographic*. None of these works is pornographic or violent. *The Fortune Society Newsletter* which can be said to advocate rehabilitation was also banned, and, although its exclusion was successfully litigated, individual copies are still confiscated.

Censorship has always had a chilling effect on free communication; abused, it has been capable of stifling it.

But perhaps a more subtle and pervasive obstacle to inmate contact with the free world is the quality of everyday prison existence. Designed for the mastery of the many by the few, it is indescribably different from life on the outside. Virtually every movement is regimented, every event routinized. Food, clothing, shelter, work, recreation, friendships and associations, hobbies, hairstyles, and fine gradations of attitude are watched and controlled by custodians who make the rules, punish infractions, and remain aloof. An inmate is allowed little or no chance to make personal decisions, either because he has seldom been thought capable of doing so or it has been deemed dangerous to allow him to try or simply because the system runs with less administrative effort in that way.

There is no privacy of body, and in spite of the "stone walls do not a prison make" whimsey, very little privacy of mind. The noise is continual, and often lights are beamed on the cells at night for surveillance. There is no way at all to withdraw from the pressures of the prison environment; for the inmate there is no private space in which to restore his personhood and his dignity—the gas chamber at San Quentin has seats for two.

None of the building blocks of ordinary conversation are found behind prison walls. There are no babies, no children, no members of the opposite sex. Nor are there kid brothers, aunts, mothers-in-law, or grandfathers. Convicts don't take trips to the beach, go to restaurants, buy new cars or fashionable clothes. The days are monotonous, typified by multiple headcounts and valid fear of harassment and exploitation by fellow prisoners and officers. Instead of information there is rumor; hustling and homosexual interplay are bases of the inmate economy; cigarettes are the medium of exchange. Little of what happens in prison makes sense to those who have never experienced it; the absurdity of the life of caged men and women is more than those on the outside can or care to grasp.

Furthermore, in many instances, prisoners actually participate in their own alienation. For sheer survival some reject the outside so that the inside might seem more real. Stripped of their former identity and encouraged in the name of rehabilitation to change their personalities radically, some adopt roles which do not work for them on the outside. The prison intellectual will not be recognized as a professor; the bully may find himself immobilized by fear when dealing with non-convicts. Still others, filled with shame and anxiety, take refuge behind the walls that confine them. There are prisoners who have refused visits and correspondence just as certainly as potential visitors and correspondents have refused them. There are, as well, prisoners who have no ties; antisocial and nonconforming in the free world, they had cut themselves off before they entered prison.

Communication is based on some degree of common experience or, at least, a desire to share experience. At a distance it requires effort and imagination. Even outside prison, relationships break down when one member goes to live in another city, changes schools, gets married, or joins the army; how much more difficult to maintain bonds when one participant is locked up in prison year after year.

Yet, in spite of the many obstacles, prisoners do communicate; and, as is evident from the number and variety of documents reviewed for this collection, they always have. They do so through legitimate channels, securing in one way or another the approbation of their guardians; or they do so illegitimately through visitors, friendly or bribed custodians, trustees, or by painstakingly concealing their messages in otherwise innocent objects. One manuscript passed the inspectors secreted in cunningly hollowed out papier-mâché picture frames.

Like any human being, prisoners communicate for many reasons: because they love the people they have been separated from and do not want to forget them or be forgotten by them; to arrange practical matters; to get books, special clothing, or hobby supplies; to protest conditions in which they live; to attack accepted social and political structures. They also communicate to get out. This last is perhaps the most pervasive because it is the most urgent. It ranges from drafting legal documents to contacting strangers who might help. Except in cases where hope has been utterly abandoned, pleas for release flavor all communication with the outside.

Prisoners also communicate to keep themselves together; the confessions, laments, justifications, and ordinary descriptions serve as an aid to self-understanding and self-development. The mental effort demanded by communication helps combat the stultifying effects of prison life and provides a vehicle for discharging some of its tensions. Prison authorities have long recognized the therapeutic value of inmate expression and in many facilities actively encourage prison magazines and newspapers. These, of course, are subject to varying degrees of censorship, but they are popular with convicts both for the challenge any publication effort entails and for the privileges working on them bring—freer movement and hours, a little more money (say, thirty cents a day instead of twenty-five), and often more private sleeping arrangements. It has also been suggested that working on prison publications affords prisoners an opportunity to demonstrate to officials and to the public that they can successfully handle the tools and conventions of free society, that they accept them, and are therefore good parole risks.

Prisoner arts and handicrafts have been sponsored by the system, too, and have been pursued by prisoners even when they are not. Writing does not work as communication for many in prison, just as it does not for many outside, and so they turn to arts and handicrafts as another form of communication. Materials are a problem, but prisoners are ingenious at using whatever is at hand. One Fort Leavenworth convict of the 1880's complained that inmates were forced to use iron eating utensils because they would steal horn or wooden handled ones to carve trinkets from. (Officials generally fear metal ones, because they can be easily fashioned into knives and pick-locks.)

Arts and handicrafts are made for souvenirs and tokens of appreciation. Sometimes they are sold for petty cash or exchanged for favors. Posters, signs, chess sets and calendars serve practical purposes; photographs and cartoons comment on the prison way of life. Often elaborate and meticulously executed, they bear witness to long hours of unfilled time and the need to embellish with some variety an otherwise gray existence. This anthology includes several examples of nonverbal communication by prisoners.

An inmate once told me that there were as many ways of doing time as there were convicts. This, perhaps, explains why, although prison living is batch living, and although most of the works that come to us do so because they have received some sort of imprimatur from free society, communications from inside convey an extraordinary sense of the individual person. Even the confessions and execution orations, further circumscribed because they are part of a ritual and are peculiarly molded by the expectations of the recipients, speak strongly of the unique human being whose testimony they are. This reaching out of the individual, the risking of self to communicate with others has a special intensity, for the essentials of existence are involved. It is in their ironical vitality that much of the significance and attraction of prison communications lies.

They fascinate too for their picture of prison life: the dreariness, the cruelty, the poverty and the humor and bravado —characteristics of perennial interest to those who do not have to suffer them and of importance to those who would reform. And they provide as well an unusual, but valid, perspective of social history; for prisons most certainly reflect the times which they serve: whether there is war or peace, what the national fiscal situation is, what are the aspirations of labor, what nationality or race comprises the poor and powerless, what public zeal there is for reform, and even what soporific is popular in the free world—whiskey, for instance, or heroin.

But the final significance of prison communications is that they are the works of fellow human beings. More than insights into life behind bars or into social history, they give us, if we allow ourselves to catch them, sudden glimpses of ourselves.

Ideally, perhaps, this anthology should have been put together by a convict or an ex-convict. But the obstacles against them are formidable. And so I have taken the role of listener and collector in hopes that, through their communications, prisoners might begin to break down the barriers that so falsely exist between them and those who are not in prison. For I am convinced that no reform and no diminution in crime is possible until we realize that the convicted and the nonconvicted comprise but one community.

CYNTHIA OWEN PHILIP

New York City
October 1972

IMPRISONED IN AMERICA
Prison communications
1776 to Attica

NOTE TO THE READER

Sources for each of the selections in this anthology appear at the end of the book.

I

The Society for the Relief of Distressed Prisoners was established in Philadelphia, Pennsylvania, on February 7, 1776 by a group of eminent charitable citizens. To encourage support from the general public it published, in the preamble to its rules, its reasons for being and its practical goals.

"The miserable situation of numbers confined in jail (particularly during the inclemency of the winter) hath often filled the humane breast with tender commiseration of their sufferings, and anxious wishes for some general plan of relief, which should be adequate to their necessities. To find many whose labour might be useful to the public, languishing out their days in a prison, when the payment of their fees would have set them at liberty long ago, must strongly urge the feeling mind to solicit their enlargement.

"But considerable sum being necessary for this desirable purpose, it was thought advisable to begin an institution on a lower scale and content ourselves for the present with relieving the most present wants of our miserable fellow creatures in the *new jail*, who are there deprived of many of those comfortable supplies they had an opportunity of obtaining in their former central situation. Who can visit that house of variegated misery, and not wish to clothe the naked shivering wretches!—To kindle a fire on the cheerless hearth and spread warmth and gladness through the damp and melancholy apartments! Who can turn from meagre want, and not supply mere hunger's cravings—or bear the sight of pining sickness on the sordid floor, and not relieve her misery! The charitable and humane will rejoice in this opportunity. . . ."

1   *Most common criminals were released from jail during the revolutionary war. There were, however, thousands of prisoners of war to
take their places. Although they did not suffer the censure of society,
they were beset by the same poor food, lack of privacy, abundance
of vermin, and longing for release as ordinary convicts. They were
warehoused in whatever structures were available from jails, sugar
houses, and churches to ship hulks. In the course of the war, thousands died of disease, starvation, cold, and the venality of their
keepers.*

*In a letter to his family in West Hartford, Connecticut, Jonathan
Gillet describes his capture during the retreat of the Continental
army after the Battle of Long Island, August 1776. Lieutenant Gillet
was subsequently confined on a British prison ship where he was
"seized violently with the disentarry and after that a slow fever," but
was fortunate not to be among the scores who died. He was then sent
to the Old Sugar House, Liberty Street, New York. On parole, he was
allowed "to walk part over the city between sun and sun" and thus
was able to report on the fate of his fellow prisoners. Gillet's health
deteriorated to such an extent that in 1780 he was permitted to return
to his home. Within a few weeks he died, showing symptoms of
having been poisoned as well as starved. His son later suffered imprisonment in the same sugar house, but he survived its rigors.*

My friends,
    No doubt my misfortunes have reached your ears. Sad as it is,
it is true as sad. I was made prisoner the 27 day of August past
by a people called heshens and by a party called Yagers, the
most inhuman of all mortals I cant give Room to picture them
here; but this much I at first Resolved not to be taken, but by
the Impertunity of the Seven taken with me and being
surrounded on all sides by numbers I unhappily surendered;
would to God I never had—then I should never have known
there unmercifull cruelties; they first disarmed me then plundred
me of all I had, watch Buckles money and sum Clothing after

3

which they abused me by brusing my flesh with the buts of there guns. They knocked me down; I got up and they kept on beating me almost all the way to there camp where I got shot of them—thc next thing was that I was allmost starved to death by them. . . .

After giving you a small sketch of myself and troubles I will Endeavour to faintly lead you into the poor cituation the soldiers are in especially those taken at Long Island where I was; in fact there cases are deplorable and they are Real objects of pitty—they are still confined and in houses where there is no fire—poor mortals, with little or no cloths, perishing with hunger, offering 8 dollars in paper for one in silver to Relieve there distressing hunger: occasioned for want of food there natures are brook and gone—they are crouded into churches and there guarded night and day. I cant paint the horable appearance they make—it is shocking to human nature to behold them. Could I draw the curtain from before you; there expose to your view a lean Jawd mortal————hunger laid his skinny hand and whet to keenest Edge his stomach cravings, sorounded with tattred garments, Rotten Raggs close beset with unwelcomed vermin. Could I do this, I say—possable I might in some small manner fix your Idea with what appearance sum hundreds of these poor creatures make in houses where once people attempted to Implore God's Blessings &c but I must say no more of these calamities. God be merciful to them—I cant afford them no Relief—If I had money I soon would do it, but I have none for myself. . . .

December 1776

2 *Famous for loathsomeness, the Jersey prison ship was anchored in Wallabout Bay off the Brooklyn, New York shore; vulgarly and aptly she was called "Hell." Formerly a fifty-four-gun warship, she was*

dismantled because unseaworthy and was one of several hulks used by the British to confine captured revolutionaries; often over a thousand men were jammed below her decks. Exchange of prisoners by opposing armies was accepted military strategy and a constant source of hope to all prisoners. This letter is from one of her angry and luckless captives.

Jersey Prison Ship, August 10, 1781
There is nothing but death or entering into the British service before me. Our ship's company is reduced to a small number (by death and entering into the British service) of 19. There is a partial cartel arrived and bro't 11 prisoners, and the names of so many as makes up that number, sent from Boston by somebody, and dam the villain that trades that way tho' there is many such in that are making widows and fatherless children. a curse on them all. The commissary told us, one and all to the number of 400 men that the whole fault lies in Boston, and we might all be exchanged, but they never cared about us; and he said the Commissionaries were damned rogues and liars.

I am not able to give you even the outlines of my exile; but this much I will inform you that we bury 6, 7, 8, 9, 10 and 11 men in a day; we have 200 more sick and falling sick every day; the sickness is the yellow fever, small pox, and in short, everything else that can be mentioned.

I had almost forgot to tell you that our morning's salutation is, "Rebels! turn out your dead!"

3 British soldiers were also imprisoned. This memorial from British officers confined at Waxhaws, South Carolina, was addressed to Major General Nathanael Greene. Greene had been appointed to the

5

*southern command in 1780 and by the end of 1781 had captured all
the British posts, except that at Charleston, South Carolina.*

Waxhaws 12th Jany 1782

We the British Officers Prisoners of War, beg leave to represent
to your Excellency the many insults and numberless threats we
have met with since our arrival in this Settlement, particularly
on Friday the 11th instant about nine o'clock at Night, when a
Party of ten or twelve Men disguised; armed with Rifles, Swords
and Pistols burst open the door of our Quarters, with presented
Arms threatening our Lives forced us into a small Out-house
where they had secured our Servants; and kept us Confined
until they plundered the House of every individual Article.

Thus deprived of every Necessary, we have to request Your
Excellency will remove us to some more civilized part of the
Country (as in this we do assure you we cannot think our Lives
secure from the many threats we daily receive) where we may
have an opportunity of supplying ourselves with Money and
other necessaries which we are now very much in want of.

Your complying with our request and favoring us with an
Answer as soon as convenient, will be gratefully acknowledged
by

Your Excellency's
Most Obedient
Very humble Servts

4 *The revolutionary war might correctly be termed a civil war, for
thousands of Americans remained loyal to the English king. Those
who failed to take an oath of allegiance to the new nation were
considered traitors; many were imprisoned, their property confiscated.
From 1775 to 1783 the Newgate prison in Connecticut, a converted*

copper mine, served as the national prison of the Continental govern-
ment. Prisoners entered by a perpendicular shaft fifty feet deep and
were confined in dripping, noxious underground galleries. It was
deemed by General Washington, who sent a group of convicted
loyalists there, a fit and sufficiently secure place for "such flagrant
and atrocious villains."

Simeon Baxter of New Hampshire, having been proscribed, ban-
ished, and deprived of his estate because of his militant loyalism, was
one of the Newgate prisoners. He became voluntary chaplain to his
fellow Tories and on September 19, 1781, delivered himself of a
rousing sermon entitled "Tyrannicide proved Lawful from the Prac-
tice & Writings of Jews Heathens and Christians." This is its closing
exhortation, advocating the violent overthrow of the newly estab-
lished government.

We have rights of civil society to restore; we have honor, virtue,
and religion, to maintain: let us therefore take the first prudent
opportunity to revenge our wrongs, and kill those tyrants, who
are lurking in every corner to spy our motions, and murder the
innocent. Their motto is, *To destroy or be destroyed.* Therefore,
let safety rouse us into action—let Fame reward the sacred hand
of him that gives the fatal blow—let his name live for ever with
Cato and with Brutus.—O how I long to save my country by
one *heroic, immortal* action! but alas! my chains and dreary
mansion, where the light of conscience reigns, without the light
of the sun, of the moon, or stars!—To you, my virtuous
countrymen, who are free of the chains with which I am loaded,
I conclude my address. It is now in your power to circumcise,
put down, those uncircumcised tyrants, and to restore yourselves
to your social rights. You know the action that will do the
business, and which shall register your names among the Gods
and bravest men. Patriotism warms your souls, and thousands
are burning with ambition to join and save your country from
Romish bondage. Make haste! for the Spirit of understanding

causeth me to speak in the language of Zophar, *Let death and destruction fall upon* Congress, *because they have oppressed and forsaken the poor: let a fire not blown consume them: if they escape the iron weapons, strike them through with a bow of steel* —for knowest thou not this of old, since man was placed upon earth, that the triumphing of the wicked is short, and the joy of the hypocrite but for a moment. And although the devils are to come down in great wrath, with power in their mouths and in their tails; although their heads reach the clouds, and though they do hurt with their tails; yet their murders, their fornication, and their thefts, shall be revealed, and the earth shall rise against them, *to feed them with the poison of asps. The vipers tongue shall pierce them through, and their greatness shall be chased away as a vision of the night. This is the portion of the wicked.*

5 *Connecticut's Newgate prison was not so secure as its reputation claimed. Escapes and burnings of the blockhouse that stood over the mine shaft entrance were frequent, caused by the laxity of the guards, according to the citizenry. They sought to correct this situation by jailing the jailer, neither an imaginative nor a successful solution.*

To the Hon. General assembly, The Humble petishen of *Able Davis*—whare as at the honerable supene court houlden in Hartford in December last I was conficted of mis Deminer on the count of newgate being burnt as I had comand of said gard and was orded to bee confind 3 month and pay fourteen pounds for disabaing orders, I cant read riten, but I did all in my power to Distingus the flame, but being very much frited and not the faculty to doe as much in distress as I could another time and that is very smaul, what to do I thot it was best to let out the prisners that was in the botams as I had but just time to get the gates lifted before the hous was in flames, and the gard being frited it twant in my power to scape them. I now pray to be Deflehaned from further in prisment, and the coust of said sute as I hante abel to pay the coust, or give me the liberty of the yard as I am very unwell as your pitishner in Duty bound will for ever pray.

Abel Daveis

Hartford Gaol January 14th 1783.

6 *America, perhaps because of its strong religious traditions, has always nurtured conscientious objectors and has often jailed them. On the twelfth of July, 1787, Norris Jones was committed to the Philadelphia gaol "for not paying a fine of six pounds imposed for Not taking the test of allegiance to this State in Order to Qualify me to Serve on a Jury for the tryal of the Courses in the Supreme Court," to which, as a Quaker, he objected. His diary reflects his struggle to maintain clearness of religious conscience against the arguments of friends who were anxious to secure his liberty on legal or civil grounds. Jones had resigned himself to a long confinement and was surprised when on the twenty-eighth of July the jailer released him to his friends; he confesses he "did not feel rejoiced at it."*

6 day [of the week, July 20, 1787] This morning my friend Jas. Thornton with 3 other friends call to see me & on informing him particularly of the case & ground of my refusal for not taking the test which was simply this—I had for this ten years been very thoughtful about it; there was always a secret something in me that could not consent to take it, although it had been several times new modeled and at present appeared very simple to some, but on looking at the

root & ground of the tests it doth appear to me that it hath not its Origin in the truth but in a party spirit & human Policy Something oposed to the Pure Truth which leads all the followers to a Compliance with the constant mind as far as consistent with their principles.

After which Jas. Thornton had a freedom to see Judge McKain. On the occasion Jas. Pemberton, Samuel Smith & James Cresson went with him & and had an opportunity with him. He was mild & treated them becoming. It was proposed to have an interview with me when he would have an opportunity of seeing the disposition I was in. He redily agreed to it and fixed on 12 o'clock to meet friends at this place near which time he came. But to their surprise found him in a very different disposition; he appeared angry and not much satisfaction expected. I was favoured to keep cool. He wanted to know my objections for refusing to take the test. I saw it would be difficult for me to convey my scruple so as for him to understand it because he is very much unacquainted with the principle which I believe restrained me; however I told him I had for some time felt a scruple in my own mind & I ever found it safest for me to stand still while that remained; but to be sure he worked & even ridiculd it as a mistaken notion, something enthusiastic but no marvel. Though he hath read law for 30 years (as he said) I believe it to be impossible to attain a knowledge of the truth through that medium. He took a good deal of pains to point out the propriety of my taking it & justified his Proceeding towards me. I told him I was neither afraid or ashamed of my objections & did not care who knew them for I did believe it was upon that Ground that Never did Deceive. The opportunity lasted above an hour & he withdrew; not much satisfaction on the whole.

This afternoon my dear mother came to see me. It had been a considerable tryal for her, but on reflection was satisfied & favoured to resign me to him who never said to the seed of Jacob "Seek ye my face in vain." I have from time to time felt the near sympathy of my dear friends many of whom my spirit hath often been nearly united with.

7 *In the eighteenth and well into the nineteenth century, executions were important public affairs, often drawing crowds from long distances and characterized by a gala as well as a pious and awesome atmosphere. An expected part of the ritual was an autobiographical narrative and a confession by the victim. These were printed immediately and were popular for their exciting and edifying details. Although these works have many similarities in form, their content and spirit are controlled by the author's personality and circumstances.*

Francis Uss tells us in his preexecution life narrative that he acquired a habit of roving early in life. Born in Strasbourg, France, in 1761, he emigrated to Philadelphia with his parents when he was a boy. He returned to Europe on his own, eventually joining the Duc de Lausanne's regiment, and sailing to America to fight in the "war between Great Britain and France." He was captured by privateers and imprisoned by the British at Pensacola. He gained his liberty by enlisting in their service, but after an arduous trek through the southern wilderness during which he subsisted on "a few herbs, never before perhaps used for food & now & then a land tortoise eaten raw," he rejoined his French regiment. Uss received two wounds in the historic Battle of Yorktown. After the Revolution he lived with his widowed mother for a short time in Philadelphia. There, because he was involved in a "fray" and "not immediately finding a surety I was imprisoned for three years with a large number of criminals; with whom no additions were made to my virtue." Released, at last, he went to New York and thence to Mohawk where he married. Finally his wanderlust led him to Poughkeepsie. Following is an excerpt from the autobiographical narrative "which he gave to a visitor a day or two before his suffering"; he was hanged on Friday the thirty-first of July, 1789, in Poughkeepsie.

11

In the beginning of the present summer my evil genius led me to Poughkeepsie, on the way to which place I committed several small thefts: On my arrival in Poughkeepsie I called at the shop of Major Billings, where the valuable articles exhibited in it, tempted me to commit the fact for which I am justly to suffer. Whatever I might have said on another occasion, while a gleam of hope remained and the expectation of pardon was not totally obliterated, I now candidly confess that of this burglary and robbery I was the sole perpetrator. No accomplice shared the guilt—no accessary divided the spoil. . . .

My life has been a life of dissipation and wickedness, and a few more revolving hours will close it in infamy. . . . Ah! me unhappy what shall I do? Writhing in agony, and convuls'd with grief, I fall amid the clanging of my chains prostrate on the floor of my dungeon and WISH a supplication to my maker: for my poor distracted mind is incapable of coherence, and the half-formed syllables die upon my tongue.

If groans unutterable, and sighs from the inmost soul have a language, mine is most pathetic.

The terrors of the approaching awful Friday rise up in fearful anticipation before me! I have realized them so often they cease to be ideal. Once more I will indulge them, and hand in hand with horror, once more walk over the gloomy stage.

After a night spent in disturbed slumbers and terrific dreams, I rise from the floor and see the gleamings of a rising sun which I never never more will see go down. The birds hail in cheerful notes the new-born day—but music to me has lost its charms, and to me the new-born day brings woes unutterable. Food is set before me; but I turn with loathing from nourishment, for what connexion is there between life and me? My pious friends surround me, and retire not, till they have wearied Heaven with the most fervent supplications in my behalf. Oh that I felt their fervor, had their faith, and enjoyed their consolations?—The day last advances—I hear the din of crouds assembled in the streets —Again there is a noise at the prison door! The massy key grates upon the wards of the lock, and grates too upon my very soul. The door recoils, and enter the ministers of justice. Pity is painted on every countenance. The sounding file is applied, my chains drop to the earth, and my limbs are once more free, only soon to be bound in never-ending obstruction.

Heavens! what are my feelings while the suffocating cord is adjusted to my throat! Death is in the very touch. . . .

8 *Abraham Johnstone, born a slave, served five masters in Delaware before he was granted permission to buy his manumission. Although free, he was jailed in Baltimore and in Dover as a runaway. He then was captured by "Georgiamen" who intended to sell him on the southern slave market, but he escaped to New Jersey where, at the time, there was more protection for free blacks. Following is part of Johnstone's message "to the people of colour," which he gave to them immediately before he was executed for the murder of a Guinea Negro. He was convicted of this crime on circumstantial evidence and, though calmly and religiously resigned to his fate, he steadfastly protested his innocence.*

Woodbury, in the County of Gloucester, and State of New Jersey on Saturday the 8th day of July, 1797

In the first place then I most earnestly exhort and pray you, to be upright, and circumspect in your conduct; I must the more earnestly urge this particular from a combination of circumstances that at this juncture of time concur to make it of importance to our colour for my unfortunate unhappy fate however unmerited or undeserved, may by some ungenerous and illiberal minded persons, but particularly by those who oppose the emancipation of those of our brethern who as yet are in slavery, be made a handle of in order to throw a shade over or

13

cast a general reflection on all those of our colour, and the keen shafts of prejudice be launched against us by the most active and virulent malevolence: But such general reflections or sarcasms, will be only made by the low minded illiberal and sordid persons who are the enemies of our colour, and of freedom: and to them I shall simply answer that if the population throughout the United States be then taken, and then a list of all the executions therein be had, and compared therewith impartially, it will be found that as they claim a preeminence over us, in everything else, so we find they also have it in this particular, and that a vast majority of whites have died on the gallows when the population is accurately considered. A plain proof that there are some whites (with all due deference to them) capable of being equally as depraved and more generally so than blacks or people of colour.

Another circumstance that renders my fate peculiarly unhappy at this crisis, is that it happens at a time when every effort is using for a total emancipation of all our brethern in slavery within this state, and that by men of exalted spirit generosity and humanity—men whose bosoms glow with philanthropy, good will to all mankind and a love of freedom that shews them to be activated by the noblest of all motives, that first great principle in true religion, "do to all men as you would be done unto."—men whose spirit rises indignant at seeing their fellow creatures whom God has created in his own likeness and endowed with immortality, held in bondage to each other, or that one human being shall have it in his power to torture and inflict innumerable pains and punishments such as his ingenuity may devise and as caprice may dictate to him on an unfortunate fellow creature who happens not to hold an equal rank in society with him tho' he undoubtedly does in creation and the eyes of the Almighty.

'Tis thence my dear friends and brethern that I esteem it so peculiarly unfortunate, as it may be made a handle of to retard the truly laudable endeavors of such generous and worthy persons. But no, I hope not, I am convinced that it cannot: for such a generous and noble work is too acceptable in the sight of God, and is founded on a basis too solid and firm to be at all shaken by such wayward untoward or unfortunate and unforseen accidents, as this proves to be, and as to the scoffs sneers and railings of the spitefully malicious or envious, let them consider but a moment that no living man knows what fate has in embryo for him to suffer, and that no man knows his length of days nor what moment death shall usher him into an endless eternity.

9 *Benjamin Bailey wrote this repentant farewell letter at about three o'clock the morning of his execution. He had first shot then struck with a tomahawk an itinerant peddler whom he had decided to rob on Machonoy Mountain near Reading, Pennsylvania.*

Reading Gaol, January 6, 1798

My dear and loving wife!

I have at last brought myself to acknowledge the truth, of the charge, brought against me, and I assure you my dear, I feel myself cas'd of a weighty burden, that lay on my mind; the struggle was great, but I acknowledge the power of God. I hope you will pardon me for so long concealing this matter from you, and at the same time, impute my crimes to the instigation of the devil: but thanks be to the almighty God, who has open'd my eyes and shewn me my error, and on whose power and goodness I now depend for my salvation. I hope my dear, you will forgive and pray for me; my sins are great and numberless, O my dear! if I had staid with you, I should not have now to implore pardon from my maker for this crime. I have seriously considered your request of the Sheriff and advise you not to persist in seeing my corps, as my dear I fear the sight will injure you, and only distress instead of comforting you, you are here alone, and I do not know that it will be proper for you to expose yourself to so dangerous an undertaking. I have my dear, made my confession to the Sheriff & Mr. Worrell in the presence of two ministers who attended me, and it is committed to writing. I must once more request you not to attempt to see my corps, altho the Sheriff told me a few hours ago he would do all in his power for you; and I doubt not but that he will perform, if you still persist in your request, I would advise you, my dear! to send some person who can satisfy you in regard to my burial. I think it needless to mention any thing more respecting my body, as I wrote my request in my last, which you may refer to. O my dear wife! forgive! forgive your Bailey, who expects to leave this world in a few hours; in firm hope of meeting you one day in heaven, where there will be everlasting Joy, world without end, Amen.

Benjamin Bailey

Courts could order that the bodies of executed criminals be delivered up for dissection; for years this was the only legal source of cadavers. Apparently it was also common practice to exhume and steal them. The day before his execution, Bailey's wife wrote this letter to the sheriff.

Dear Sir,

I do with humble prostration, throw myself at you feet, and plead for two favours, that is to dig Bailey's grave deeper, than is common for such graves to be dug, for my brother is not come, and I mean to set on his grave, until I think he is safe from the surgeons. And the other is, dear Sir, to keep his body untill the crowd is a little gone, that I can come, and see it. . . .

10 *Imprisonment for debt was commonplace in the eighteenth and well through the nineteenth century. As the following selections indicate, debt struck high and low alike; the punishment suffered under the debt laws was particularly discouraging because it was so obviously self-defeating. This supplication, dated October 23, 1795, from New Ark Prison, describes a typical debtor's plight.*

Dear Sir,

I beg leave to pass by your hand the enclosed Petition to the honorable the Legislature of New Jersey, praying that an act of insolvency may be pass'd in my favour. The said petition is a Just narrative of well known facts, to all the people that was acquainted with me in Morris and Summerset Counties to which I beg leave to refer you. Since I left that part of the County I have lived in *Paterson* and it is also well known that I took every prudent measure in my power in order to obtain a living for me and my family, by teaching school all the Week and on the Sabbath for those that worked in the Cotton Mill printing shop & also all my Children down to Six years old was employed by the Society. My Wife also kept not less than eight or ten Boarders on an average, but this time twelve month the Town and Vicinity of Paterson was very much afflicted with the ague and fever, and my Boarders among others was visited with that disorder which rendered them unable to pay me their Board of course I was obliged to get provision on Credit thinking that when they got well that they would pay me in order that I might pay the debts contracted as above; but to my great loss and disappointment they were unjust and unfaithful and made their escape without ever bidding me farewell, and to be short is the very cause of this my imprisonment. I hope Sir you will think it your duty to use your influence to have said act pass'd in my favour which will be a means of restoring a distress'd prisoner to his small family in

order to contrive and help my poor distressed wife and children.
I hope the favour will never by forgot by your distress'd hum
servt.

John Wright

N.B. I have eight Children but two of them is put out, to get
their living. J.W.

11 *Convicts delight in setting up mock courts. Sometimes they serve a*
practical purpose and sometimes they are for amusement; but they
are also used to maltreat fellow inmates. Occasionally prisoner or-
ganizations become so strong that it can be said that they, rather than
the keepers, run the prisons.
   The prison court of the New York debtors' prison was ostensibly
devoted to ensuring the "peace, order, and Harmony of the Hall."
It was based on an elaborate constitution and had an appellate
division for the reversing and mitigating of sentences. According to
the following minutes, it dealt severely with dissidents.

Monday Decr. 26th. 1796. 11 o'clock

This court opened agreeable to adjournment & the following
Sentence was pass'd on Joshua Snow who stands convicted of
having Behaved in an unbecoming manner By erasing his name
from the Book of the constitution.

Sentence

   The Court determine that Joshua Snow be Sentenc'd to close
confinement in his own Room for one Month; that during that
time he shall not be permitted to walk the Hall except for the
discharge of the evacuations of nature or a discharge from
Prison. That he is hereby excommunicated from the Benefits of
the constitution and declared unworthy the conversation of the
Members of the Hall who are desired not to hold any

conversation with him unless upon private Business, and that in his own Room. And that he cannot hereafter be permitted to sign the constitution again until after the expiration of his Sentence and a public concession be made in open court to the satisfaction of all the members.

At a Special Court held on the Twenty-fourth day of April 1797,—A notification having been fixed up in the Hall signed Isaac Sherman recommending a Meeting in a Mode Unauthorized by the Constitution and tending to disturb the Peace Order and Harmony of the Hall—

The court esteem it their Duty to recommend it to all persons, who are Friends to the Established Constitution and the preservation of the Public peace, not to countenance any illegal Meeting by their Attendance but in case such a Measure should take place to keep within their respective rooms: in Order that the real Friends of the Constitution, and of Order may be distinguished from those who after having solemnly pledged themselves to support it, are now Endeavouring to subvert it—

•

Like many administrations, the debtors' was prey to bribery.

New York April 21st 1797

Gentlemen:

I charge Mr. Davis my fellow Warden with having acted as follows, to wit: That on the Morning of the 20th instant Mr. Mitchell put Dirt into the Hall after the Morning Sweeping and on the said Davis's seeing it informed the said Mitchell that he would complain of him to the Judges unless he the said Mitchell gave him two Glasses of Gin in which case he would say nothing about it—Therefore as such conduct may be attended with the most serious Consequences against the

19

Harmony of the Hall I pray that you will order the said Davis to appear before you to answer to the charges &c.

> I am Gentl your Obt St.
>
> Edwd M. Mills

We the Subscribers do concur in the above application for a Court.

Lack of privacy in the close quarters of prison is a constant source of irritation. In the early prisons inmates were not separated by degree of offense, age, or sex. From the following note it is apparent that the men could not resist criticizing the women, nor the women complaining about the men.

Mrs. Frean's Complaint against Ellison

. . . whereas the said Charles Ellison at divers Days and times between the 12th and the 19th Day of this present month of August did pronounce and utter the following false scandalous and defamatory words to wit: you, meaning the said Margaret Frean, are a dam'd infamous Bitch, a Dam'd Lyor, a damn'd faggot, a damn'd infamous Woman &c. and further that the sd Charles Ellison did on the Evening of the 19th make or suffer to be made such a Noise and disturbance in his Room as entirely to disturb her peace, & the Company with her; and further that after the People of the Hall are all gone to Bed, he uses such insulting Language to his Wife by damning & cursing her, that her Rest is thereby disturbed and her Peace interrupted, and She is prevented for several Hours from Sleeping and sometimes by that means her Rest broken for a whole Night: all which doings of him the said Charles Ellison are of evil Example and tend to disturb that Peace Harmony & good Order which ought to Subsist in every civilized Society. all which she prays may be enquired into by the court.

> Margaret Frean

12　*In 1798 Robert Morris, the financier of the American Revolution, was arrested by a small creditor; it was later estimated that he owed three million dollars. He spent the next three and a half years in the Prune Street debtors' apartments (variously spelled Prun or Pruen), an annex of the Walnut Street prison. He was finally released under the new bankruptcy law. Ironically, when yellow fever was ravaging Philadelphia, vagrants and disorderly servants who were likely to crowd and endanger the health of the inmates of the city prison were housed in the shell of his marble palace, which he had commissioned the famous architect L'Enfant to build, but was unable to complete because of his financial embarrassment. Throughout his troubles Morris remained strongly attached to his family and they to him. Such was the faithfulness of Mrs. Morris and their daughter Maria that they continued to visit the prisoner even though they had to pass through streets piled high with coffins.*

This letter is addressed to John Nicholson, Morris's partner and friend, who was soon to join him in the Prune Street apartments. The illness was undoubtedly yellow fever; unhappily, the child William died.

Philadelphia Octr 9th 1798
(Pruen Street)

J. W. Nicholson Esqr.

Dear Sir

My son William continues very Ill & they send me word this morning that he had a restless night. I am not alarmed for his safety because I cannot believe that He is destined to be taken from us so soon. I had before had the same thought that you express as to the similitude of Mrs. Nicholson's & his disorders and I expect that likeness sufficiently fullfills the omen of the dream, I hope however that it may continue a little longer until they both recover perfect Health in a short space of the same time. I had yesterday strong expectations of being at Home with my Family last night, nothing prevented it but extreme caution

& timidity of the Sherriff. I wrote to him on Saturday asking a Copy of the Chief Justices letter he did not receive mine untill Sunday nor did I get his reply with the Copy untill yesterday, when to my astonishment I found the Chief Justice had written as fully to the point as I could expect or wish, notwithstanding which the Sherriff thinks there is a doubt as to his safety, and says there ought to be none. I shall try this day with the help of Jno Baker & some of the Lawyers to remove his doubts & if that is effected I shall once more get into the Bosom of my Family & at a time when they need that Comfort which my presence will administer.

I am DrSir yours &c Robt Morris

13 The Forlorn Hope *was America's first inmate publication. (Morris and his partner Nicholson are said to have written a newspaper to while away the hours at Prune Street, but it was not for general circulation.) It was founded by William Ketelas, himself a debtor in the New York City prison, and it was oriented toward reform of the bankruptcy laws. It carried such diverse items as a reprint of George Washington's Farewell Address and the advertisement for "a well recommended WET NURSE, with a fresh breast of milk." Here is a contribution from the Newark prison with which, apparently, New York had close connection. Characteristic of prisoners' saving sense of the absurd, it appeared in the first number, March 24, 1800.*

Mr. Printer,

The genial influence of our country's Natal day, pervaded the walls of this enchanted castle!

Such distinctions as our confined situation permitted, were paid to this auspicious day. Our procession was not very far, and thank God, not very numerous. The banner borne for the occasion, was a tattered pair of breeches, *which has seen better days*, displayed on a constables staff with inverted pockets . . . the top of the staff was decorated with an *empty purse*, and a label inscribed TEKEL.

14 *This letter is from Philip Williams, imprisoned in the Washington, D.C., jail for possession of a counterfeit bank note, to John Parrish, abolitionist of Philadelphia. It describes the anguish of black and poor prisoners.*

City of Washington
5 May 1806

Sir,

I have lately read a Pamphlet bearing your name written on the subject of Slavery—In every feeling breast it must excite the mingled emotions of sympathy for the cause of suffering humanity; & resentment against cruel oppressors, & avaricious tyrants, who encourage, or are concerned in this nefarious traffic in the blood of fellow men. Excuse my warmth for I have within the last 3 or 4 years been a witness to *so much* misery of this kind, that I cannot suppress my indignation against those who pamper their voluptuous vices at the expense of the liberty, blood & lives of *beings* far less unworthy than themselves.

I rejoice that these poor and afflicted people/the Blacks/ have at last got so good an advocate to plead their cause at the bar of public opinion—It is not to be less wondered at than regretted, that this meritorious work has not been sooner undertaken. Had my situation in life, or humble abilities, admitted me to attempt such a task; I should long since done so. . . . My own unhappy distiny has placed me in a situation, where I am obliged to be an eye witness to so much of this barter & cruel treatment of my fellow creatures, that I almost forget my own wretchedness, in contemplating that of others—In short Sir, as my principal object in writing you was to acquaint you with some facts which may be of use to you in your future speculation I cannot fulfill that purpose without disclosing to you the circumstances of my own confinement—Painful & mortifying is the task of doing so —Next month I shall have been 2 years incarcerated within the walls of a cell of 8 feet dimensions. . . . The charge against me was badly supported; or the Jury could not have been 24 hours in making up the verdict of *guilty*—that since my conviction the inhabitants of my place petitioned the President for my release, & testifies their belief of my being *"Not guilty"*—that the man of whom I received the note has written the Marshall & offered to swear that he let me have the note as good and that I knew not of its being bad. But the Judges say as these facts were not established in court while on trial, no advantage can now be derived from them—Several applications have been made to the President & Judges in my behalf; & I have offered in case of being emancipated before my sentence is out, to go into the army or navy, or if necessary as a condition, to leave America forever—But all my entreaties have been in vain.

Was it not that I owe money, of which I have no means or prospect of paying, I could be much better reconciled to my fate—I owe perhaps 1000 dollars, & am now worth not a cent. However, when I look round me and hear the pitious moan of so many fellow Prisoners, & fellow creatures, doomed to perpetual servitude, & oppression's bloody scourge, I feel reason to bless *GOD* for the small portion of hope which yet remains with me; & which these poor creatures cannot enjoy—Since my confinement here, more than *"One Hundred"* of the poor blacks have been taken out of this one prison, manacled, & driven off to Georgia, by these monsters in human shape call'd *"negro Buyers"* or *"Georgia-men."* Several members of congress have been concerned in this traffic, during the late session— They were often at the Jail—I saw them, but can only recollect

one of their names, which is *Elias Earle* from S. Carolina—
These members pretended they were only buying for their own
use; but it is notorious that it was for speculation—It is
common to see at the starting of these *droves* (I have often
seen it with anguish) children parted from their parents,
brothers from sisters, & husbands from wives, with all the
agonizing tortures, which separations are calculated to produce
—Some are brought here by their masters in order to punish
them, and by way of aggravating the punishment, they are
usually whipped most unmercifully, sometimes before coming in
sometimes while here, & others after taking them out—

Last summer Thomas Jenkins had a fellow who runaway—the
fellow who went away has a brother nam'd *Ellick* a black smith
who works in the city of George Town & belongs to the same
man, Jenkins, and on a bare surmise (which turned out to be
entirely unfounded) that Ellick knew where his brother had
gone to, he was tucked up & lacerated in a most inhuman
manner, & kept in jail upwards of a month to make him tell
where his brother was—But he protested to the very last, that
he knew not of his brother's going away, & the event proved he
told the truth—Just before that happened, there was a Virginia
Gambler from Richmond who was in George Town, and has a
servant called *Michael.* For some unguarded expression that
Michael unthoughtfully let fall, his master a Mr. Robinson
brought him to jail, & after he had been about a week confined,
come one day with a new cow hide, stript Michael, tied his
hands behind him & made him lie down in his cell & after
whipping him till one side was raw, made him turn over so as to
have a fresh place to cut until the miserable sufferer was
covered with wounds & blood from his neck to his posterior all
round his body—The cries of that unhappy victim, & the
merciless execrations of his barbarous Master, filled me with
emotions, not easily described, & never to be forgotten—Several
men of colour have been confined here as Runaways who were
free, & after being kept 5 or 6 months in jail & proving their

freedom, cannot obtain the least redress for their wrongs—The magistrates would not even grant a release only on condition of their Jail fees being paid by themselves. But on application to the Judges of the circuit court, their Jail fees have been remitted—but no recompense for lost time, nor hardships of imprisonment—Among those who have thus suffered I can recollect the names of Randall Allison, of Baltimore, Joseph R. Lee, of the same place, James Frazier of Philadelphia, & Thos. Johnston of Charleston, none of whom remain'd in prison less than 4 months & from that to six months—The two latter were Seamen, & had it seems faithfully served the U. States on board their Frigates, and after the frigates returned from the Mediterranean & the crews discharged, these poor fellows were seized by the cupidity of the constables who get a fee of 3 or 4 dollars for taking up any black man who is without free papers, & these had lost their free papers by accidents at Sea—Tho' it was manifest to the constables themselves that they were free men, & it was well known to them at the time of taking them up—Nor is this the only kind of wrong which shelters itself under the law—Those very laws which are made for the protection of innocence are often perverted into instruments of severe & unjust punishment on that very innocence it professes to defend—Of this I have also seen many instances—I will mention only two—One Peter Lee a yellow man of this District a very religious man was accused of stealing a piece of cloth, and after being imprisoned nearly a year, his prosecutor either ashamed or afraid to meet him in court, never appear'd against him, & he was turned out without even a hearing.

In one of the coldest nights of last January a poor man in this place, imprudently (tho' it is believed with no criminal intent) took a fence rail off another man's fence, to make a fire for a chilly wife & child—For this trifling offence he was dragged off to jail the same night where he still is, & will remain till next court which is in June or July—having a helpless wife & child with little else to depend on than the uncertain events of charity—He was a poor man, who had not been long in the city and could not give security for his appearance in court—so that he must suffer about 6 months imprisonment. then probably taken out and flogged, & saddled with all the jail court charges, say 100 dollars, only for taking in a suffering unguarded moment, what no Jury would value at 20 cents—His name is Casper Wagner a Dutchman from your state—I could mention many other instances of a similar nature, but these may suffice—It is all legal I suppose; but to *me*, it does not appear right—Our Jail itself is not an such humane establishment as yours—Here is no Benevolent Societies to superintend prisons or Poor Houses—Everything is left to their keepers—If they are good, 'tis well - if bad 'tis of no use to complain—The jailor gets no salary—He is allowed 20 cents daily for each prisoner's maintenance—Out of that allowance arises his profits & of course the cheaper he can find them the better for himself—

Such are the passing & past events at the centre of government in this land of boasted liberty & equal rights.

There is not a circumstance I have narrated, but admits of the most incontrovertable proofs, & they are by no means exaggerated in the relation—I shall make no apology for the intrusion on so large a portion of your time, not for obtruding on your attention so many tales of woe—To one so feelingly alive to the unjust sufferings of others as you are, I hope no apology will be necessary—

These papers will be handed to you by a young man of this city who tomorrow sets out to Philadelphia on a visit to his mother, & will be there for three or———

Should you wish to make any reply or inquiries he will be——— a safe hand. He is a———who has paid me much attention since my imprisonment & has promised me to see you himself— ———enquiry you should think me entitled to your

commiseration, probably an application from your Society to the
executive in my behalf, might procure my liberty—

The best services of my future life would not be an
equivalent of the value of such a favor done for me—

I remain Sir
Most Respectfully
Philip Williams

Mr. Parrish
Author of a Pamphlet
   on Slavery
Favor of Mr. Gideon

15 *Roberts Vaux, the recipient of the ingratiating letter that follows,
was a Quaker reformer and civic leader of Philadelphia whose philan-
thropic activities ranged from advocating vaccination to founding an
asylum for the relief of persons deprived of their reason and of schools
for the deaf, dumb, and blind. For many years he was corresponding
secretary of The Philadelphia Society for Alleviating the Miseries of
Public Prisons (established 1787, a postwar successor to the Society
for the Relief of Distressed Prisoners, which was disbanded when the
British entered Philadelphia and took over the jails in September
1777). Vaux is considered a major American penologist. He was also
a victim of prisoner Van Horn.*

Philadelphia prison Ot the 11th 1818

Respected Sir;

   I hope you will pardon the boldness I have taken in
   addressing you in a letter respecting my situation.
I have been confined three years and am destitute of any friends
to assist me in my distress—and having every reason to believe

that you are willing to bestow your humanity on me—I now as one of the most unfortunate men—implore your assistance relative to my release from prison. The charge for which I was justly convicted for I acknowledge was of the blackest dye yet when you remember the time that I have suffered in prison I hope it will amply compensate for the crime committed it is unnecessary to made any promises relative to a better course of life I shall only add that I now see the folly of dissipation and look back on the time lost that might of been devoted to the benefit of myself and the comforts of others and should your mercy be extended towards me so far as to make application to the Board of Inspectors in my behalf I shall ever feel bound under the strongest obligations for your kindness.

I am your most obediant servant,

John Van Horn

Attached to the letter are Vaux's notes on his encounter with Van Horn:

The author of the annexed letter (John Van Horn) about dusk on the evening of the 7 month of 1815 committed a robbery upon me on the Germantown Turnpike Road nearly opposite to the country seat of Joseph Parker Norris about two miles from the City of Philadelphia. I was riding in my Chair with my wife, having been on a visit to Dr. Wistar at his summer residence in Roxburry back of Germantown. The circumstances of the robbery were these—

The horse was seized by the bridle & stopped by a robust fellow, who held him securely, at the same instant Van Horn approached the side of the Gig, placed a pistol to my breast, & demanded my money, I told that I had no money with me —he answered *"Your money—no delay—no delay"*—My wife remonstrated with much firmness & said that she had all the money in our possession, & would furnish it she then was proceeding to hand him some small change notes in her purse —when he said *"Your watch Sir, no delay—your watch or I will blow you through!"* "Give him the watch said Margret" I obeyd the demand, he took the watch and suffered us to pass on—Some days after this event, T. R. Peters Esq. & his friend Curwen were robbed by the same Highway men, & soon taken, tried & convicted. Van Horn was sentenced to 10 years confinement.

16 *Captain Elam Lynds, veteran of the War of 1812 and erstwhile hatmaker, was the first principal keeper and the second warden of Auburn Prison, New York. He was chosen to supervise the construction of the new penitentiary at Mt. Pleasant (Sing Sing), using convict labor from Auburn and Greenwich prisons, and he became its first warden. He is credited with originating the Auburn penal system whereby inmates worked together in complete silence and were lodged in separate cells at night; he introduced the single file and lockstep and encouraged the use of the disciplinary whip. His administration was successful from a security point of view, but it was despotically maintained; he once complained that he could not get keepers of sufficient ruthlessness. Lynds's arrogance was a thorn in the flesh of the commissioners who appointed him. In 1830 he was accused of cruelty and mismanagement, but was exonerated; in 1838 he was indicted for want of humanity and resigned his wardenship. Lynds's fame springs from the fact that under the contract labor system he had shown that prisons could return a profit to the state, a goal that has never lost its appeal for prison officials, legislatures, and the public at large and that has been the source of much mal-treatment of prisoners.*

To the Honorable G. C. Verplanck, in Assembly, Albany.
State Prison Auburn
21st April 1823

Drsir

I have rec'd yours and with pleasure give you all the
information I can obtain from the convicts as there are but few
of them that I have any personal knowledge of. I am compeld
to take their word for the fact and their personal pride will be
an inducement to them to say that they can read & write if
they can, but there is not more than 12 or 15 men here who
profess any information obtained by reading and altho they say
they can read and write they can bearly do so, and that not
intelagibly and may be said to be allmost as illiterate as if they
could do neither. From your report to the legislature I hear you
have been lead to believe that thare is a much greater degree of
severity exercised towards the convicts in this prison than the
facts will warrant much has been said here and abroad of the
treatment received by these men and from the language of your
report I should suppose you had heard something of what has
been said, but I do assure you thare is no rule of this prison but
will comport with the best feelings of humanity and that no
man is ever punished but on conviction of braking some one of
those rules. They are perfectly intelagible and every man mad
acquainted with them and is not held accountable till he fully
understands them, but when he is so made acquainted with
them he is sure of being punished for every breach of them. at
the same time he is told that we do not punish for the love of
the duty but from a sense of justice as man that is orderly and
industrious has no more of punishment here than what arises
from his confinement. his food is ample and of good quality his
clothing is comfortable and his labour moderate, he is confined
in a separate cell at night and strictly prohibited from having
any conversation with his fellow while at work. his Cell is
sufficiently lighted for him to read and he is furnished with a
bible and made to read it if he can. hence all the ideas they get

31

here are drawn from the Holy Scriptures and those connected with their Labour. much of the opinion of great severity towards convicts here arises from the men in Solitude which common citizens are not allowed to visit and they imagine much worse than fact. and not infrequently give their imaginations to the public as truth. The inspectors have made the four ministers of this Vilage Chaplains to the prisons and they preach alternately and————the convicts separate and together which gives them an opportunity of knowing if anything was wrong in their treatment and I believe that no class of men would sooner have their feelings enlisted on the side of humanity. I have requested of them their opinions on the subject, which three of them have given me (the fourth being absent) and which I take the liberty of enclosing to you. I have taken the liberty of writing this much to you Sir as you appear to take some interest in a subject that is undoubtedly extremely interesting to the public but verry little understood by them. I believe the greatest fault in all these establishemnts is too great a laxity of discipline. The regulations of all are good in the main but are not enforced it is verry easy to prevent these men from corrupting each other (which is a great complaint against the institutions) if the police is good. There has been a goodeal said about our using the rod too much I do not know whether you have heard of it but from an observation that fell from you at Rockwell while I was there I thought you were of the same opinion. now Sir if you would spend one week with me here I have no doubt but I could convince you that on the score of humanity it is the verry best mode of punishment that could be adopted in the first place it prevents a thousand little offenses that are punished in other prisons by confinement in the dungeon for from one to ten days when a man is angry he will tell you he dont care for your dungeon and bread and water but if he knows that the rod is ready and will be promptly inflicted he will learn to govern his temper and we have men here now that have not had a particle of punishment for more than a year that when I came to the prison were a terror to the keepers but are now perfectly docile and industrious. but that like all power to punish ought to be in the hands of men whose judgement and behaviour are unquestionable.

> I am with———respect your most obedient
> verry Humble Servent
> E. Lynds Agent

17 *A pre–Alcoholics Anonymous testimonial.*

> 11th Month 23d 1824

Estemeed Friend. I take the liberty under Serious imprisonment to open my thoughts to thee Respecting Some Reports about my being intemperet. I have very Seriously reviewed the subject and conclude that in order to put it out of the power of any body to charge me with the like again I have Seriously & Solomly concluded to bare my testiony fathfully against the use of any kind of Spiritous Lickquers except it may be Directed for Medical Purposes.

Believe me to be Sincere in the foregoing Remarks I belive & kind Providence has furnished us with the best kind of Drink, that is Water it will certainly better Qualify us for our Lawfull evocations than any kind of Strong Drink if what I have said will have a tendency to Remove unfaverable inprestions witch I hope it will and thou Will blive to be Sincere I remain thy Friend and Well Wisher.

> Nathan Atherton

18 *Women have always comprised a small percentage of the nation's prison population and it has been easy to overlook them, especially because both the judicial system and the correctional system have*

been peculiarly male provinces. In the nineteenth century women were most commonly arrested for stealing, drunkenness, vagrancy, and infanticide, and were usually held as objects of scorn by their keepers as well as by law-abiding society.

Philadelphia Prison   June 12th 1825
Mr. Morgan: Sir I hope you will please to take my Case into consideration the articales that was found in my house that you clame as your property I bought at Constables sale in Locust above Tenth St. the man who owned them got me to go and buy them in for him and when he got the money he would pay me and take them agane or I might sall them agane, and make my profits they were seized and sold for rant. Robinson was the Cryer and a young man who writes in Mr. Barkers office was Clark of the sale. I have gave you a statemint of the perticulars and I hope Sir you will please to reflect that Im heare seprated from my Child you are a parent your salf and I leve it to you to judge how a mother feels when toren form hir Child (not five yers old) thare fore Sir I cannot write any more on the Sudgact but Leave it to you to Judge of my feelings yours &c &c

Ann Price

NB if you are willing to lat me go out of prison you will please to write a note Diracted to the Inspactors please give it to the barier of this yours &c &c

Ann Price

19   *Counterfeiting was especially rife throughout the United States between 1812 and 1819. Most banks printed and issued their own notes and they had so proliferated that it was impossible to keep up with the variety of bills in use although "guides to sure notes" were issued*

weekly. By the 1820s making one's own money had become a more exacting task and many counterfeiters were jailed. But according to W. A. Coffey, prisoner in the New York State Newgate prison from 1819 to 1822, "The glave of justice merely lops off withering branches, and does not cut off and destroy the root." He reported that there were sixteen wholesale dealers in New York City alone. They neither retailed nor passed "cogniac" themselves, but sold it to jobbers who disposed of it in small quantities to others, who, in turn, put it in public circulation. These last, poor with families they could not support, got caught while the wholesalers pocketed the profits with impunity. The following letters are from "sharpers" who were apprehended in Pennsylvania. They are addressed to Mayor Joseph Watson of Philadelphia.

Philadelphia Penitentiary Dec. 24th 1825

Honored Sir

        I humbly trust you will pardon my thus addressing you to solicit your powerful & benevolent influence in my behalf, and to implore your Honor in the name of Mercy, Humanity and Justice to aid a wretched & truly penitent man. "To err is human To forgive divine" And that I have and, yes greatly err'd I acknowledge in humility and with penitence—but have I not Sir done much to retreive my errors —have I not disclos'd facts, and those of more importance, than any other man ever did placed in my unhappy situation. I came forward voluntarily to your Honor & made a full disclosure of my own guilt, with the guilt of others, and through the information I then gave, some have already been apprehended & are in all probility at present suffering for the crimes they had so long practiced with impunity. Your Honor will please to call to mind that I was but once before you, and what came to my mind at that time, I related without reserve—every question which was asked me I answered freely & without hesitation. I have since stated other circumstances to Mr. McClain and also

procur'd three different plates which have been given up to your
Honor. Permit me respected Sir to intreat you to call to mind
all I have done & to consider it with your accustom'd Justice
and benevolence and to weigh the services I have render'd to
the Commonwealth with the injury I may have done. And may
I not also implore your Honor to throw into the scale my truly
distress'd situation, with that of a young and unprotected wife
whose affliction is equal if not greater than my own. . . .

Chas. Mitchell

Arch Street Prison July 4th 1825
    Mr. Watson Sir I have been better than six months in this
prisson and am gitting verry bad off for Shirts and Shoes as I
have been so unfortunite as to have all the best of my close
stolen from me in this place and my unfortinate family is in
such sircumstances as not to give me any assistance nether have
I any friens in some distance from heare to asist me to any
thing therefore I hope that my case will be well considered this
cort and I also hope that my ginarel carector will be shone to
you before I am cauld to cort and if it is I will be satisfeyed for
I should be glad to have you know my former carecter, and thee
I must acknowledge that I was Draged into this unfortinate
Charge and was not awaire of the Consequences arising from it
and I assure you that this is the first Charge that Ever came
against me or ever can come and I hope that it will be the last
as I ever have indeavred to live industres and honest life heare
to fore.
    And I expect that you have sean some time agoe a large
quantity of five Doller Bills on the Camdan Bank also and you
have sean ar will soon sea tens and twentys on Wilmington
Bank also all of wich is executed within the County and City of
Philadelphia from your humbel Servant

Aaron Howell

II

On June 2, 1826, the Boston Prison Discipline Society presented its First Annual Report "with devout acknowledgements of gratitude to Almighty God, for his continual smiles, and the unexpected success with which the efforts of this society have already been crowned."

In pursuit of the society's object "to wit; the improvement of public prisons" the managers had visited prisons in the thirteen states and the District of Columbia. They found the Female Department of the Baltimore Penitentiary and the New Hampshire Penitentiary outstanding examples of good management: the matron of the former having turned a deficit of $1,099.51 into a profit of $492.51; the superintendent of the latter changing a loss of $4,235.61 to a gain of $6305.44. But

"At Auburn, we have a more beautiful example still, of what may be done by proper discipline, in a Prison well constructed. It is not possible to describe the pleasure which we feel in contemplating this noble institution, after wading through the fraud, and material and moral filth of many Prisons. We regard it as a model worthy of the world's imitation. We do not mean that there is nothing in this institution which admits of improvement; for there have been a few cases of unjustifiable severity in punishment; but on the whole, the institution is immensely elevated above the old Penitentiaries.

"The whole establishment from the gate to the sewer, is a specimen of neatness. The unremitted industry, the entire subordination and subdued feeling of the convicts, has probably no parallel among an equal number of criminals. In their solitary cells, they spend the night, with no other book but the Bible; and at sunrise, they proceed in military order, under the eye of the turnkeys, in solid columns, with the lock march, to their workshops; thence in the same order, at the hour of breakfast, to the common hall, where they partake of their wholesome and frugal meal in silence. Not even a whisper is heard; though the silence is such that a whisper might be heard through the whole apartment. . . .

"The feelings which the convicts exhibit to their religious teacher, as he passes from one cell to another, are *generally* subdued feelings. Sometimes, however, a man is found who hardens his heart and exhibits his obduracy even here; but the cases are comparatively few. The want of decorum, of which the commissioners of the State of New York complain, in their visit to the city Prison, where they were met by the bold staring of the prisoners, after they left their work, to gaze at them, and by looks, whether in smiles or in frowns, which indicated an unsubdued and audacious spirit, in the culprits; this is never seen at Auburn. The men attend to their business from the rising of the sun to the setting of the sun, and spend the night in solitude."

20 *The judge who sentenced Robert Bush hoped that in his year of
solitary meditation awaiting trial he had had time for reflection on
the justice of his punishment. Apparently he had. Bush used a
mixture of tobacco (which he swallowed) and opium (how obtained
and administered not known) to kill himself two days before he was
to be hanged in Springfield, Massachusetts. He was thought to be
under the influence of opium when he shot and killed his wife in
Westfield. These are his last protesting words, "written and delivered
to a fellow prisoner, a few hours before his death."*

Whoever reads the trial of Robert Bush, for the murder of his
wife, ought to know whether there was not some cause for this
cruel deed, and whether this was from malice and revenge
altogether or not, and her treatment to him while she lived with
him and after, and the situation she lived in where she died, in
order to know how much pity to grant, and not to waste it, for
it is verry scarce the right sort. There are a number of sorts of
pity in our little world—it is a pity that a man must be tried for
his life by the solicitor General and support judges and jurors to
look on—it is a pity that she did not treat her husband well for
it would saved trouble—it is a pity that it was all the comfort
she took was in tormenting her husband—it is a pity that she
should go and live with another man that had no other family
but a small boy—it is a pity that her husband should not had
patience and wisdom enough to have borne her insults and not
troubled himself, but he must had the patience of Job to face it
all and possess a regular mind—it is a pity that a man should be
sentenced to death from the testimony of them that know
nothing about the case—it is a pity that there are so few men
in the world where there is so many people—it is a pity there
should be so few Christians in the world where there is so many
Church members—it is a pity there should be so few justices
where there is so many esquires—it is a pity that our judges
should deal so largely in judgment and so little in justice and

mercy—it is a pity but no wonder that the people mourn when old maids rule—it is a pity that honest men are so often talked about when then are so seldom seen—it is a pity that there is so many people in Westfield in favor of single men and married women living together—it is a pity that religion should be so often talked about and so seldom practised—it is a pity that the Courts of Hampden county should keep men in jail on fines of equal sums and equal crimes from three to six months each. This I should call a court of judgment where justice dont enter.

21 *In the early 1820s, the slave states, growing increasingly fearful of the blacks, adopted a more aggressive attitude toward oppressing them. In most of the South whites were even forbidden to teach slaves how to read or write. There was a continuing undercurrent of defiance, but the first real insurrection of slaves against their masters occurred in Southampton, Virginia, in 1831. It was led by Nat Turner, a religiously inspired, visionary activist. Before the revolt was put down by state militia and federal soldiers and sailors, fifty-seven whites and up to a hundred of the rebels had been killed. Twenty-eight insurrectionists were convicted; thirteen were hanged, including the only woman, and the rest were deported. All of those executed, except Nat Turner, were given a decent burial; his body was delivered up to the doctors. It is said that they skinned it and made grease of the flesh, saving the skeleton for display and making souvenirs of the hide.*

Turner describes the beginning of his "great work of death" on the twentieth of August, 1831, in the following passage taken from his prison confession.

Since the commencement of 1830, I had been living with Mr. Joseph Travis, who was to me a kind master, and placed the greatest confidence in me; in fact, I had no cause to complain of his treatment to me.—On Saturday evening, the 20th of

August, it was agreed between Henry, Hark, and myself, to prepare a dinner for the men we expected, and then to concert a plan, as we had not yet determined on any. Hark, on the following morning, brought a pig, and Henry brandy, and being joined by Sam, Nelson, Will and Jack, they prepared in the woods a dinner, where, about three o'clock, I joined them. . . .

I saluted them on coming up, and asked Will how came he there; he answered, his life was worth no more than others, and his liberty as dear to him. I asked him if he thought to obtain it? He said he would, or lose his life. This was enough to put him in full confidence. Jack, I knew, was only a tool in the hands of Hark. It was quickly agreed we should commence at home (Mr. J. Travis) on that night, and, until we had armed and equipped ourselves, and gathered sufficient force, neither age nor sex was to be spared (which was invariably adhered to). We remained at the feast until about two hours in the night, when we went to the house and found Austin; they all went to the cider press and drank, except myself. On returning to the house, Hark went to the door with an axe, for the purpose of breaking it open, as we knew we were strong enough to murder the family should they be awakened by the noise; but reflecting that it might create an alarm in the neighborhood, we determined to enter the house secretly, and murder them whilst sleeping. Hark got a ladder and set it against the chimney, on which I ascended, and hoisting a window, entered and came down stairs, unbarred the doors, and removed the guns from their places. It was then observed that I must spill the first blood. On which, armed with a hatchet, and accompanied by Will, I entered my master's chamber, it being dark, I could not give a death-blow, the hatchet glanced from his head, he sprang from the bed and called his wife—it was his last word, Will laid him dead with a blow of his axe, and Mrs. Travis shared the same fate, as she lay in bed. The murder of this family, five in number, was the work of a moment; not one of them awoke. There was a little infant sleeping in a cradle, that was forgotten until we had left the house and gone some distance, when Henry and Will returned and killed it. We got here four guns that would shoot, and several old muskets, with a pound or two of powder. We remained for some time at the barn, where we paraded; I formed them in line as soldiers, and after carrying them through all the maneuvres I was master of, marched them off to Mr. Salathiel Francis', about six hundred yards distant.

22 *Gustave de Beaumont and Alexis de Tocqueville were commissioned by the French government to study the penitentiary system in the United States with a view to discovering models of reform. They completed their work in 1832 and in 1833 their report was published in the United States. It is a valuable work not only for the extensive research and careful perceptions of the authors, but also for the notes of the translator, Francis Lieber, distinguished editor of the* Encyclopaedia Americana *and author of many articles on penology.*

Lieber was a supporter of the Pennsylvania system of solitary confinement with labor because it made possible ease of classification, prevention of corruption, and short sentences. It rendered severe discipline unnecessary; convicts were not embittered or irritated against mankind when released. The recorded recidivism rate was low as was the in-prison disease rate. Lieber's arguments provide a balance to the publications of the Boston Prison Discipline Society which militantly advocated Elam Lynds's Auburn plan of daytime associated work in complete silence, combined with nighttime confinement in single cells. The attractions of this system were relative cheapness of prison construction and promise of profits; but it required many keepers and terrible punishments to insure silence, order, and productive labor. In practice there was often more than one man to a cell.

In the course of their study de Beaumont and de Tocqueville spent two weeks interviewing inmates of the new Eastern Penitentiary near Philadelphia; they were allowed into all the cells and left alone with the prisoners. In spite of having been doubly translated, the interviews retain a freshness that vouches for their authenticity.

Cell no. 28: This prisoner knows how to read and write; has been convicted of murder; says his health, without being bad, is not so good as when he was free; denies strongly having committed the crime, for which he was convicted; confesses to have been a drunkard, turbulent, and irreligious. But now, he adds, his mind is changed: he finds a kind of pleasure in solitude, and is only tormented by the desire of seeing once more his family and of giving a moral and Christian education to his children—a thing which he never had thought of, when free.

Ques.   Do you believe you could live here without labour?
Ans.   Labour seems to me absolutely necessary for existence; I believe I should die without it.
Ques.   Do you often see the wardens?
Ans.   About six times a day.
Ques.   Is it a consolation to see them?
Ans.   Yes, sir; it is with joy I see their figures. This summer, a cricket entered my yard; it looked to me like a companion. If a butterfly, or any other animal enters my cell, I never do it any harm.

Cell No. 56. Has been convicted three times; has a feeble constitution; has not been well during the first months of his stay in the penitentiary, which he atttributes to lack of exercise, and sufficient current of air. He has been brought [transferred] to the penitentiary at his own request; he loves, he says, solitude; he wishes to lose sight of his former companions, and form no new ones: shows his Bible, and assures us that he draws his greatest consolations from this book.

Ques.   You work here without reluctance: you have said to me that this was not the case in the other prisons, in which you have been imprisoned; what is the cause of this difference?

Ans. Labour is here a pleasure; it would be a great aggravation of our evils, should we ever be deprived of it. I believe, however, that, forced to do it, I might dispense with it.

Cell No. 22. A negro of thirty-four years; has been convicted for theft once before; eighteen months here; health pretty good.

Ques. Do you find the discipline to which you are subject, as severe as it is represented?

Ans. No; but that depends upon the disposition of the prisoner. If he takes solitary confinement bad, he falls into irritation and despair; if, on the contrary, he immediately sees the advantages which he can derive from it, it does not appear insupportable.

Ques. Have you been imprisoned already in Walnut street?

Ans. Yes, sir; and I cannot imagine a greater den of vice and crime. It requires but a few days, for a person not very guilty, to become a consummate criminal.

Ques. Do you think that the penitentiary is superior to the old prison?

Ans. That is, as if you were to ask me, whether the sun was finer than the moon?

Cell No. 61. Age fifty-five; enjoyed a comfortable fortune previously to his imprisonment; was a justice of the peace in his county. He was confined for having killed his wife's lover.

This prisoner, who speaks French, seems to be occupied but by one idea—that of obtaining his pardon. We never could make him speak of any thing but of his trial, and the causes which produced it. He is drawing up a memorial to the governor; we were obliged to hear a part of it, and to examine with him his papers. He is sentenced to a long confinement; he feels himself old, and only lives upon the hope of soon being delivered. This man seemed to us to believe in the efficiency of the kind of imprisonment which he suffers. He finds it peculiarly fit to correct the guilty, with whom, however, he takes good care not to number himself.

23 *This coverlet was woven in 1838 by an inmate of Auburn, New York, prison. The wool was home grown, carded, spun, and dyed in Stony-brook Long Island, by Ann Garret. The coverlet was exchanged for apples and dried peaches.*

24 *Thomas L. Nichols was a brash young muckraker who in June 1839,
at the age of twenty-three, tangled with the mayor of Buffalo and
landed in the Erie County Jail, charged with libel. During his sentence of four months he composed a journal as "a resource, a past-
time, and a pleasure" and also, he confesses, for future publication.
The diary contains vignettes of county jail life—a mock trial of new
prisoners by old ones; the ball-and-chain gang returning from work
on the streets; a little boy crying outside for his mother who is inside
because she refused to testify—but mostly it is made up of glimpses
of Nichols's love life, perhaps because he did not want the public to
associate him with common criminals. For as he "bleached in his cell
as they bleach celery," more and more pretty young ladies were
attracted to his barred door. There were Julia and Miranda and
Rosalie, and others whose names he never found out. Here is part
of a letter to the irresisting Rosalie; he preserved it in copy in his
journal.*

Do you perceive what I am at? I write to pass time, to fancy I
am not alone, to imagine I am looking into your eyes, and
talking to you. I write because I would write to someone, and
that some one should be a lady; and you, for the moment—not
very gallant, but I can't help it—*happened* to be uppermost in
my mind; and so, for that reason, and that only, I write to you:
no that *is* candid, but it is not quite true, for I write in the
expectation of getting an answer.

Are you astonished? You need not be. I am between four
goodly walls, and fear nothing. Should you pout, what care I?
unless you pout through my iron grated door, and then I will
pout back again, and we will see who can pout the hardest; for
that, you know, or might know, or ought to know, is a game
two can play at.

Then, if no "extraneous influence" is brought to bear upon
you, I shall have an answer; and that, in fact, is the real object
of my writing. The secret is out. I would like to have you call
and see me, but will not urge it. It is not a very pleasant place

for a young lady to call; nor, you may think, for a young gentleman to stay. Indeed, I want to hear from you, and I want to hear the news—all the dear gossip—how Mr. Nichols is in jail, "poor fellow"—"too bad"—"good enough for him," etc. You have time, every qualification; we are on the right terms precisely—that is, a little friendly or so; not particular, but might be—that is—indeed I don't quite know how it is. But there is nothing to prevent you from writing as much as you please, as often as you please, and as familiarly as you please. . . . I'll be generous. I'll not take any advantage.

25 *The Mormons and the Missouri militia had for some time been engaged in what can perhaps best be described as a civil-guerrilla war. In 1838, when Joseph Smith, Jr., Prophet of the Church of Jesus Christ of Latter-Day Saints, was charged with treason and murder and confined in the Liberty Jail in Clay County, he said, "Our treason consisted of having whipped the mob out of Davies County, and taking their cannon from them; the murder, of killing the man in the Bogart battle." While incarcerated he composed an epistle to the Church discussing its present situation and its strategies for the future. Parts of this letter were regarded of such special value that they were placed in the Doctrine and Covenants of the Mormon church. Such an excerpt is presented below.*

And again, we would suggest for your consideration the propriety of all the Saints gathering up a knowledge of all the facts and sufferings and abuses put upon them by the people of this state; and also of all the property and amount of damages which they have sustained, both of character and personal injuries, as well as real property; and also the names of all persons that have had a hand in their oppressions, as far as they can get hold of them and find them out; and perhaps a committee can be appointed to find out these things, and to take statements, and affidavits, and also to gather up the libelous publications that are afloat, and all that are in the magazines, and in the encyclopaedias, and all the libelous histories that are published, and are writing, and by whom, and present the whole concatenation of diabolical rascality, nefarious and murderous impositions that have been practiced upon this people, that we may not only publish to all the world, but present them to the heads of government in all their dark and hellish hue, as the last effort which is enjoined on us by our Heavenly Father, before we can fully and completely claim that promise which shall call Him forth from His hiding place, and also that the whole nation may be left without excuse before He can send forth the power of His mighty arm.

It is an imperative duty that we owe to God, to angels, with whom we shall be brought to stand, and also to ourselves, to our wives and children, who have been made to bow down with grief, sorrow, and care, under the most damning hand of murder, tyranny, and oppression, supported and urged on and upheld by the influence of that spirit which hath so strongly riveted the creeds of the fathers, who have inherited lies, upon the hearts of the children, and filled the world with confusion, and has been growing stronger and stronger, and is now the very main-spring of all corruption, and the whole earth groans under the weight of its iniquity.

26 *The Cherokees were a settled, highly civilized Indian tribe whose extensive country covered the mountain lands from the southern Alleghenies to northern Georgia. That the United States recognized them as an independent nation with its own laws and customs did not prevent their white neighbors from coveting their land and, under*

the Indian Removal Act of 1830, from driving them to painful exile west of the Mississippi.

The constitution of the Cherokee nation, adopted in 1838, when the last of their people had arrived in Indian Territory, provided for a judicial system similar to that of the United States. Trials were held before duly appointed judges, with counsel for defendants and prosecutors; a jury of twelve was selected by the defendant from among twenty-four of his countrymen. Archilla Smith, a Cherokee known for recklessness and violence, was accused of the murder of another Indian and was tried in December 1840 under the nation's new, written, and published legal code. Politically, he belonged to the faction that opposed the established government so that great pains were taken that he receive a fair, even generous, trial.

The following speeches were reported by J. H. Payne, a white writer who was an intimate friend of the Cherokee Principal Chief, John Ross. He was present throughout the trial and at the execution which took place on January 1, 1841. On the ninth and final day of the trial, the jury, having reached its verdict, took its place and the Chief Justice addressed the prisoner.

Archilla Smith, after a most careful investigation, you have been found guilty by a jury of your country of having murdered John MacIntosh. You know the penalty of your crime; and, upon its enormity, it is unnecessary for me to dwell. But the last awful duty of my office now remains to be fulfilled; and would to Heaven you had been proven innocent instead of guilty, that I might have been spared the sad necessity of pronouncing upon a fellow-citizen, who has flung away such opportunities of being useful to his country, the last and dreadful sentence of the law: which is, that you, Archilla Smith, be retained in close custody until the expiration of five days hence, when you must be taken, on the first day of January, 1841, to the place which may be assigned for your execution, and at the hour of twelve noon, then and there be hanged by the neck until your body is dead, and may the Lord have mercy on your soul!"

Archilla Smith, "with perfect composure, and in a clear, firm tone," replied in Cherokee:

"You are every one of you old acquaintances of mine, Jurors. You have been several days engaged about my difficulty. But I have no hard thoughts against any one of you, Jurors, nor Judge, against you. I believe your object has been that my trial should be a fair one. I have, therefore, only one thing to say; and that is to the Judge. If the laws of the nation provide any course whereby I or my friends can petition the Principal Chief for my safety, so as to enable me to live again in peace, I would call upon the Judge to grant me that privilege. At the same time, I am aware that we are all alike subordinate beings. God is our Creator and he is my Master. If he has so ordered that I am to live on earth no longer, I am satisfied; and shall feel no disposition to complain of any one; for I was present, Jurors, when you were called to swear before your Creator that you would do justice in my case, and I believe you have decided according to what you think justice."

The Chief Justice, in consultation with the Foreman of the jury and some of the jurors, examined the law and the recorded testimony and found they could not sanction a petition to the Principal Chief for pardon. These are Archilla Smith's last words, spoken to the assembled crowd from the wagon which served as his scaffold.

"Friends, I will speak a few words. We are to part. You will presently behold how evil comes. I do not suffer under the decree of my Creator but by the law passed at Tahlequah.— Friends, you must take warning.—I think, perhaps, that my being hated has brought me to this. No man can hope every time to escape; and the third I have been overtaken by the law. But avoid such practices.—I suppose I was preordained to be executed in this manner. I am ready to die. I do not fear to die. I have a hope, there, to live in peace. I should not have shed tears had not the women come here to see me—I have no more to say."

27 *George Thompson was studying for a ministry to the Indians at the Mission Institute, Ohio, when he was arrested with two friends for attempting to entice Missouri slaves across the river to freedom. "At first they branded us with the name of Mormons, than which* Abolitionists *excepted, there was not a more odious name in Missouri," Thompson reported in his prison narrative. Sentenced to twelve years, he served, by his count, four years, eleven months, and twelve days—seventy-nine pretrial days in Palmyra Jail, the rest in the state penitentiary at Jefferson City, Missouri.*

The latter institution was run as a money-making enterprise, auctioned off to the highest bidder; in 1842 its use and profits brought fifty thousand dollars for a ten-year lease.

Thompson viewed his confinement creatively, if "not exactly taking the slave's place, yet it is suffering with him, and for him, and will shorten the time of his bondage." He never stopped preaching against slavery. This prophecy of doom was penciled on the bottom of a drawer in his cell stand to enlighten future prisoners.

"Woe to them who decree unrighteous decrees, (such as slave laws,) and establish iniquity by law," (such as buying and selling men—parting wives and husbands, parents and children—causing men to work without wages, the hire of whom crieth unto the Lord for vengeance.) Let every one engaged in this system of hellish iniquity be afraid and tremble, for the judgments of heaven hang over their guilty heads, and will quickly fall upon them unless they repent.

O! man, "flee from the wrath to come." "Escape for your life." Ruin is nigh. "What thou doest, do quickly;"—for unless you humble yourself before the eternal God there is no heaven for you, but an awful, eternal hell.

The slaves are God's poor. All their sufferings are noticed by Him—every stroke of the whip is recorded—every groan counted—and every tear bottled up by their Maker, to be brought up against you at the solemn judgment. How will you answer? What will you say for yourself? You will be speechless.

I pity the fate of a slave-holder. If there is a low place in hell, an enlightened slave-holder will occupy that place. He will be cursed by men and devils.

I pity the children of slave-holders. They are trained up for oppressors, upon whom God will pour the "blackness of darkness" forever and ever.

I pity a patrol. This office is cruel, low, mean and heart-hardening.

Dear stand,—You have been very kind to us in our confinement. For your valuable services we are very thankful. As we are now about to leave you, we bid you farewell, and send you into the world a single-handed abolitionist, to preach deliverance to the captive, to rebuke men for their sins, and warn them of their danger. Cry aloud to high and low, rich and poor—spare not. May you do much good and be protected. We commend you to the mercy of the people. May many of the oppressed be delivered by your means.

I pray some eye may fall upon it, and that good may result by the blessing of the Lord. "How great a matter a little fire kindleth."

28 *There are suicides in every prison. It is the duty of the state to protect its prisoners from taking their own lives and often great pains have been taken to revive the condemned so that they might be properly executed by the law rather than by their own hand. But prisoners are ingenious and when their anguish is great enough they find a way to end it. In 1971, an inmate at Folsom Prison, California, wrote of a friend who, out of loneliness, despair, and fear, had hanged himself in a punitive strip cell: "He wanted to live so desperately that the thought of being killed snapped his mind." The note below was inscribed on the bunk of a prisoner who, beaten beyond endurance for attempting to escape, drowned himself in the river. It was used as an illustration of the sorry state of prison discipline in the first annual report of the Prison Association of New York, 1844.*

To whom it may concern. I cant stand to be flogged. to Day I Die. first farewell all my friends now am unwilling to own that such a vile outcast you ever new I would not but for the flogging that I cant take I am sorry for what is happened but alas it is too late

   I thank Mr _____ for his kindness to me since I have been here tell Mr _____ not to be so fond of punishing his fellow creatures he will have to give an account sometime. feed the molatters & show mercy

A Judson

29 *The Reverend James B. Finley was chaplain of the Ohio Penitentiary in 1846 when he wrote: "At eight o'clock this morning (May 31) I preached to the females in prison; and there appeared to be some prospect of a work of grace among them. But no one, without experience, can tell the obduracy of the female heart when hardened and lost in sin. As woman falls from a higher point of perfection so she* *sinks to a profounder depth of misery than man." He did, however, include these two letters in his* Memorials of Prison Life, *a reformist work, drawing much material from his personal journals.*

The first letter was written by a woman confined in the Ohio Penitentiary to her husband in the Indiana Penitentiary.

Ohio Penitentiary, July 29, 1846

My Dear and Beloved Husband—I received your letter, written through the warden of the Indiana prison, which gave me to know that you are alive and well. I cannot express the satisfaction I felt to think that you had not forgotten our little children, though I had begun to think that you had forgotten your unfortunate wife. I am well; but, O, what must I say about our little ones, that are scattered—we know not where! My heart bleeds, while my eyes flow with tears. I have tried to find out where they are. When I was arrested my sister had the charge of them; but not being able to support them, I suppose she had to put them out. Two of them, I have learned, were sent to the orphan asylum; but our daughter was bound out by the overseers of the poor. I was arrested on the third of May and lay in jail until August, when I had my trial, and was sentenced for three years. My mother died the day I was sentenced; and my sister says that my poor old father cannot long survive the stroke. O that I could see him, and throw myself at his feet and ask his pardon! It might be some comfort to him; for I have no doubt my mother's death was caused by my misfortunes; and now my dear old father's gray hairs must go down in sorrow to the grave! O, will my God and my parents forgive me, a poor, broken-hearted sinner! I want to see you. I want, O how much! to see our children. My dear husband, will you excuse me for not writing to you sooner? My apology is that I thought you had sorrows enough of your own, without being doubly weighed down with mine. You may have cast me off; but I thank God you are spared, and that you will soon be at liberty to look after our more than orphaned children. I should rejoice to be spared, also, to see you all once more together. Then, I think, I could suffer to be cast off or to die. I am not without comfort. Although in prison, I have a *kind* warden; and we also have a fine, fatherly minister, who preaches to us every Sabbath. I have been treated with the utmost kindness since I have been here. Let me again say, I hope I shall be spared to see you again face to face.

Your wife, L.

Of the second letter the Reverend Mr. Finley wrote: "The following is the opening paragraph of a letter written by a female prisoner, a young and rather beautiful woman, to her mother. As this daughter of sorrow was never married, her sin will be partly apparent from her own words; and the remainder of it was only the fruit, or natural consequence, of what the reader may here see. May her example be a warning to her sex!"

Ohio State Prison, July, 1846

My Dear Mother,—You cannot tell how I long to hear from you. You were never in my circumstances—no, you were never such a sinful, wretched, afflicted, abandoned being as I am; and so you cannot conceive my misery. How I weep to see some of you—my parents, or the children, and particularly my own unfortunate little boy! O, my mother, will you come and see me? Bring father with you. Or if you have cast me off, and refuse to see me, send me my babe, that I may look upon it. He knows not yet that he has a living mother, and yet one that is dead to him. Should he live to years, what will his feelings be toward me, when he thinks of his wretched mother, of what she has done and suffered, and of the disgrace in which she brought him forth! O my innocent, but disgraced and suffering child! Forgive your erring mother the fault of your unhappy fate! And

55

you, my parents—it breaks my heart to think I am bringing your gray hairs in sorrow to the grave. . . . But let me name another thing. I fear, I daily dread, a worse separation—a separation that can never be repaired. You are the followers of the meek and lowly Savior; and heaven, my dear parents, is sure to be your home. But when you arrive there, and find many of our family in that eternal resting-place, of the virtuous and good, where, O where, shall be your sinful, unfortunate, and sorrowing child! Ah, mother, it behooves me most, whatever you may think of me, to seek God's pardon, and prepare for another world. If you cannot, without too much pain, see me here, I trust that, by God's help, I shall be prepared to meet you where sin, and disgrace, and shame, and sorrow will never come.

Your erring child.

30 *The Anti-Rent Wars began in the Hudson Valley on January 1, 1838, when the tenant-serfs of the Van Rensselaer grant objected to paying the annual tithe to the lord of the manor on farms that they could not buy, but that they had worked under perpetual lease for generations. Supported by workers who were unemployed as a result of the completion of the railroad and the Erie Canal and the financial panic of 1837, and led by a group of local professional men with ties among the Free Soilers in New York City, the movement spread by 1844 to the Livingston grant, including Columbia, Dutchess, and Delaware counties. When called to action by their tin dinner horns, the anti-renters donned a calico Indian disguise, purposely reminiscent of that worn for the Boston Tea Party; the up-renters armed the sheriffs with warrants and called on the state militia for guns. There were many jailings. The leader of the anti-renters, Dr. Smith A. Boughton, or "Big Thunder," was incarcerated in irons in the Columbia County Jail, the building guarded by a hundred troops. Morti-*

mer Belden, or "Little Thunder," was imprisoned with him. Though racked with consumption, Belden cheered himself and his fellow inmates with songs improvised to the accompaniment of his fiddle. The example below was published in the July 9, 1845, issue of the anti-renters' weekly journal, The Albany Freeholder, with this introduction.

The following lines will be read with interest owing to the quarter they come from. We presume that "chaining to the floor" and some other matters are poetical licenses, excusable considering the feelings and the circumstances under which the poet wrote. It is not possible that they would chain the prisoners to the Floor.

THE PRISONERS IN JAIL
(Lines composed in the Columbia County Jail, July 9, 1845.)

There is Boughton, and Belden, and many beside,
They are quite clever fellows, or else they are belied,
For what they are in jail, I scarcely do know,
But it is base at the best—well, let it go so,
    In these hard times.

The sheriffs will out with their array of men,
The County will find them what money they spend;
They will seize upon prisoners, and into the cell—
If there's anything worse, it must be in Hell,
    In these hard times.

And there they will keep them confined in the jail,
Without any liberty for to get bail;
They will do as they please in spite of your friends,
And God only knows where this matter will end,
    In these hard times.

But the sheriff, and others, who go in the huddle,
I'm fearful are getting themselves into trouble,
For unless they keep themselves somewhere near strait,
They will be twich't at the eye at a h-ll of a rate,
    In these hard times.

But we are prisoners in jail—our cases are hard,
They look all around to keep on their guard,
Their feet fast in irons chained down to the floor,
They are pretty sheriffs what can they do more,
    In these hard times.

And as for the jailer he's a man of renown,
He spends all of his time in ironing them down;
He says for their keeping they don't get half pay,
Although he gives them but two poor meals a day,
    In these hard times.

The judges and jurors are a very fine crew,
They take the poor prisoners and drive them right thru;
The sheriffs will falter, all hell they don't fear,
They will bring them in guilty if they prove themselves clear,
    In these hard times.

They will send them to jail, and there for to lie,
On bread and cold water, or else they must die;
Or else down to Sing Sing and there for to dwell.
For twenty-five dollars they would send us to hell,
    In these hard times.

The District Attorney is a handsome young man,
He spends all his time in laying some plan,
And as for the sheriff he is a man I despise,

He will go to the governor with his mouth full of lies,
    In these hard times.

He seizes upon property, and that he will sell,
And drink by the way he can do very well;
He will do anything that will profit himself
For Uncle Sam has to pay him as well as the rest,
    In these hard times.

And as for their counsel they seem to be clever,
They tell them fine stories—make all things fair weather;
But it is for money they go as you're all well aware,
And without it they don't care a d—n how we fare
    In these hard times.

But there is the doctor I like to forgot
Still he is the meanest of all the whole lot;
He says he will cure them for half they possess,
And when they are dead he will sue for the rest,
    In these hard times.

Although he says the old jail is very filthy,
And the jailer must clean it or else he will see,
The prisoners are fast declining, and the jailer is to blame,
If he don't do his duty he'll report him very soon,
    In these hard times.

But I think now it's time to finish my song,
I can prove all I have said if you think I've done wrong:
For they are prisoners in jail without any bail,
And I think they don't like this lying in jail,
    In these hard times.

31   *Convicts look forward to holidays, ironically especially the Fourth of*
      July and Thanksgiving, when there are games or other changes in the
      daily routine and the food is a little varied; Christmas, perhaps, is
      clouded by wistful memories of hearth and family. Deprivation of
      expected privileges on holidays is considered a particularly spiteful
      form of punishment. The words of this song were composed by
      William Bradley and the music by his brother James. Both were
      convicts in the Massachusetts State Prison where it was sung to
      celebrate Thanksgiving Day, November 26, 1846

That spirit of love on the earth still abiding,
    And soothing adversity, sorrow and pain,
Now visits the captive tho' weak and backsliding,
    And raises the fallen to virtue again.
            Yes! here the gospel's light
            Shall break thro' sorrow's night
And Satan bound souls be released from his chain.

O! ye who have toiled in this vineyard neglected,
    Our gratitude deep future life shall declare;
Still call back the erring, still cheer the dejected,
    And Heaven will prosper your labor and care.
            Soon will the Saviour's voice
            Make all your hearts rejoice—
"I was in prison, ye came to me there."

Great God! in thy mercy accept our thanksgiving,
    Cleanse, pardon, and guide us as onward we
        move:
And when we shall pass from the land of the
        living,
    Receive us through Jesus to mansions above.
            Tho' thus divided now,
            Around thy throne to bow,
And join the loud anthems of wonder and love.

Phillippi's dark dungeons with anthems are shaken, And notes of thanksgiving peal thro' the night air; Oh! what can such joy in a Prison a-

waken? the friends and the spirit of Jesus are there;

there, angel mercy paints, 'mid rising, rising songs of saints, the rainbow of

there, angel mercy paints 'mid rising, rising songs of saints the rainbow of hope on the cloud of despair.

hope on the cloud of despair;

61

32 *James Clay was jailed for lascivious conduct with Miss C., a young lady who distinguished herself about town by wearing the Bloomer costume; advances in dress unsanctioned by fashion have always been looked upon as a threatening breach of social order. She was sentenced to four months or fifty dollars and Clay chivalrously paid the fine. He got six months or two hundred dollars and petitioned constantly and unsuccessfully for his release; the lascivity, he declared, was entirely in the hearts and minds of the judges. Clay was a vegetarian and opposed to liquor and tobacco; and he wanted to join an association, possible the Oneida Community, where he could form freer relationships with members of the fair sex, but his wife wouldn't let him. From the following writings, composed in the Augusta, Maine, jail in 1853 and 1854, it is evident that he was a serious champion of women's liberation.*

It is regarded as a shame, and a disgrace, that a woman make known her pure, godlike love, if she be possessed of such a virtue, in the degradation of the race. And she must blunt the passion, and perhaps blot entirely out the highest attribute of the Deity in her kind, and wait for a companion until some one comes along by chance who fancies her, perhaps solely for her external appearance; perhaps for a legacy she is to inherit, or may be because he cannot be better suited, or get whom he wants when, in fact, their souls are entirely unfitted for each other, and she, of course, must accept if he be not as repugnant as the swine; for the world is a chance-game with her, and she may never have another opportunity of marriage, and will not only have to live alone unloved, but will have to bear a reproach almost approaching to scorn, that is often heaped on the unmarried of her sex; and, further, she may be driven to the most abject slavery for a sustenance; . . .

The disparity of the pay between male and female labor serves to degrade one sex, which is also the degradation of the other. The virtues of either are dependent upon the virtues of the other, and the virtues of both on their equality and independence. It is certain that the dependent situation of the female can do no less than effeminate the race. But it is a shame that there is necessity for an appeal to the selfishness of man, in this Christian land, for the rights of woman! Have not our mothers, sisters, our wives and daughters, rights, natural rights, to be pecuniarily independent with us? Answer this, ye Christian sons, brothers, husbands and fathers! I say, answer in so the God that rules in and reigns over you, and no longer rob and enslave the gentler sex, because, forsooth, heathen nations have done it before you.

From barbarism to civilization there is every degree of disparity between the condition of the sexes; and when we attain to Christianity, we *will* then find them equal, free, and independent.

Now, though the wife and mother, by her industry, sustain the whole family on the mean pittance that custom awards her for her service, still the husband, like the southern slave-master, may own the whole. But this law and custom is being very much modified in our present day. The change, though imperceptible to those who move with the mass, is great.

It is a little rainy to-day, and I have been sitting at my window, alternately reading, writing, making toys for the children that visit me, and watching the church-goers as they pass and repass to and from meeting. One thing that particularly strikes my attention is the "draggle-tails," as I call the ladies' long dresses, dragging in the mire, or being held up half-knee high, to save their being soiled; sometimes occupying both hands to furl the enormous spread, and then leaving a skirt or two to be entangled about the heels, performing the office of fetters. The asp-like waist beneath, which is compressed into half its proper dimensions, the internal organs making every respiration for life but a feeble effort, and the bearing down of the heavy skirts on the naturally delicate and now enfeebled abdomen, and the delicate little foot crippled with tight shoes and corns, and the tallow-like countenances and premature death,—the certain result of all this,—and then the charging of all to Divine Providence;—when I behold all this, I am led to exclaim, in the language of my old school book, "O, the folly of sinners!" I wish these ladies could see the mothers and daughters of Modern Times or of the Oneida Commune, in their neat short dresses and pants, and hear them tell of the ease and comfort when compared with the long ones; they would be disgusted with their fashionable death, and flee from it as they would from the bottomless pit.

Truly, as ever, James

33 *The United States mail has always been an attractive target for thieves, from the casual loner to organized gangs; it is especially vulnerable to depredations by its own employees.*

A. C. N. was a postmaster in a large city in upstate New York who resorted to mail embezzlement to pay his debts. Since he could not put up bail and was facing a sentence of ten years at hard labor, he thought it best to escape. He was visited often by his relatives and they were of such high respectability that the jailer did not search them as he should have. Among the effects referred to in the letter below were: sundry files, saws, and chisels of the best material and workmanship; a large roll of putty to conceal saw marks in case a second night's work was required; and an empty bottle of laudanum —A. C. N. had drugged his cellmate under the guise of curing his cold; he was apparently accustomed to guiding his fate.

Sunday night

Dear Sir

Intelligence of a very discouraging nature, informing me that my approaching trial is not to be postponed on any account, impels me to make my way out of this place to-night.

Before doing so, however, I hope to thank you for your kindness to me. I am also indebted to Dr. M. for his attention to my comfort, and I regret that interests of the highest importance require me to take a step which may lead some people to find fault with you. All that I can say about that is, that I have been fortunate in eluding your vigilance as a public officer.

The effects I leave behind me should be sent by express to my friends in P——, who no doubt will pay all expenses incurred by me while I was with you. Any letters coming here may be forwarded to me at P.——, that is, after awaiting a week when my brother is to be at that place.

With a renewal of my acknowledgements for your goodness, I remain

Respectfully yours,
A. C. N.

To J. Price Esq. Sheriff &c.

34 *Greed, rivalry, and pressure from without to be self-supporting have driven many wardens to turn their prisons into sordid sweatshops. Such was the case at the Connecticut State Prison at Wethersfield in the 1860s. Inmates were let to contractors by the warden for about forty-five cents a day, while free labor commanded up to two dollars. The income was applied to the upkeep of the prison; graft and brutality were common, profits were expected.*

Gerald Toole, one of the "Catholic horde" who, according to indignant Anglo-American taxpayers, were filling the country's alms-houses, asylums, and jails, was imprisoned for life for having set fire to his liquor shop in order to collect the insurance money. Toole resisted the prison's rapacious despotism, and because he had been persecuted and flogged for not having completed an impossible task of twelve pairs of boots a day, he mortally stabbed Warden Daniel Webster in a fit of uncontrollable passion.

The following excerpts are from Toole's autobiography, which he wrote before he was executed for the killing.

I had not been long here when I found out that we were treated more like dogs than human beings. We had an instructor whose name was John Chickering, a resident of Hartford, and one who has already served a term as convict in the prison, but is now the instructor. He learned the trade of shoe-making while confined as a prisoner. The old saying, "put a beggar on horseback and he will ride to the devil" was truly exemplified in this case . . . when I tried to mend a pair of pincers, in doing which, not being conversant with the manner of doing it, made them worse; for this trifling offense I was dragged round the shop by my hair by that wretch Buck, and I have seen him use men in a much more tyrannical manner. . . . If we stopped to wipe the perspiration from our faces we were ordered by Chickering to "let 'em run," as we were only killing time by stopping to wipe it off.

. . . At this stage of the proceedings, Josiah Buck came from his desk to my bench, and asked me how many pair I had done. I replied, "Ten, or very near it." "Can you," said he, "do two more pair to-night?"—meaning before six o'clock. I then asked him what time it was. He said it was half-past five. I said, "I could not do two pair in half an hour, but I think I can do one more boot, which will be a pair and a half more than I have done as yet." "But," said he, "can you not finish your case of boots?" (The last words were uttered in a grinning sarcastic manner). . . .

On entering the dungeon, the doors had all been closed. With a sullen aspect and a flash of the eye, Webster told me to "strip off". . . . Deputy Fenton stood by, with his mounted cane in his hand; Webster also had his in the same position. . . .

Having my coat and shirt off, Webster ordered me to turn

around and place my hands on the wall, holding them up as high as possible. This done, he drew out the piercing and cutting "cat" and laid it on to my shoulders with all the dexterity and force of an enraged barbarian who has long had practice in the same school. . . . Again and again the poisonous lash cut up the flesh, and then the unmerciful tyrant, still thirsting for my blood, drew the bloody cords and sunk them in my back! The pain was excruciating; it was piercing beyond conception. . . . I had read of instances where the surgeon looked on, to see if the victim was capable of bearing more; in my case there was not a surgeon, but a *butcher* in his place. . . . Ere the last two blows fell, Webster exclaimed, in all the bitterness of his heart, "Now will you make a case of boots to-morrow—now will you make a case of boots?". . . [Toole failed to do so.]

At this stage of the proceedings, Webster turned to me, and in a surly, dogged tone, said, "Go on!"—meaning, to the dungeon. I turned round in that desperate state of mind to go, but when Webster took his heavy mounted stick to drive me on faster, (for I was no way inclined to go,) I then drew the knife from my pocket, threw my left arm around his neck, and plunged the knife in his abdomen,—although I could not tell exactly where I had been so excited, but I have heard it described as the place. At that time had Webster twenty lives, I should have taken them, I became so exasperated.

35 *The letters and diaries of the early Civil War prisoners seem to concentrate on two main themes: the possibility of exchange, thus freedom, and the men's surprise at finding themselves required to supply their daily domestic wants. Sheer survival became more important as the fighting wore on, and camps were horribly overcrowded, supplies scarce, exchange curtailed.*

Prison-Life in the Tobacco Warehouse at Richmond *(not the*

more famous Libby prison, which was actually in a ship chandler's warehouse, but the structure on the southwest corner of 25th and Main streets used by Messrs. Liggon & Co. for the manufacturing and storage of tobacco), was the first account of Confederate imprisonment to reach the north; it was published in Philadelphia in March 1862. Ball's Bluff Prisoner, Lieutenant William C. Harris of Colonel Baker's regiment wrote it "to lessen the tedium of my lengthy imprisonment" and "to recall to my fellow prisoners the varied incidents of our domestic economy in the Tobacco Warehouse." He smuggled it out "sewn securely in the lining of an overcoat."

After breakfast, washing of clothes is the order of the day. With coats off, sleeves rolled up to the shoulder, soap in hand, bucket on bench, many a poor fellow may be seen rubbing, scrubbing, grumbling, hands sore, shoulders aching, tugging away at his soiled under-clothing. He realizes for the first time in his life the domestic importance of wash-day at home.

Clothes are to be mended, buttons to be sewed on; and the busy tailors may be observed in every conceivable position throughout the room. Yonder officer manipulates a needle. See how awkward he is! He is sewing a button on his coat: now he has sewn the skin of his thumb to the cloth, now he pricks his finger, now pulls the thread from the needle. But—agony on agony!—see him threading that needle. Now he has it!—no:— try again, misses it;—try again—yes, surely he hit it then:—alas, no! and his steward comes up and threads it for him. That young lieutenant on his right is putting a patch of red flannel on his blue pantaloons. Surely he has invented a new stitch, for they are diagonal, oblong, angular, up-and-down, sideways and backwards; and the patch—ladies, did you ever hear of such a thing?—is put on bias and octagonal! When he reaches home, that patch will become one of the household treasures. How the old women will make it one of the mysteries of a tea-drinking! "See, here is a patch my boy Jimmie sewed on in 'Richmond prison,' " his fond old mother will say, holding the unmentionables up before a knot of admiring friends.

From old blankets nice pantaloons grow—a prison-adage as infallible as the school-boy's "From little acorns great," etc; and the scientific lord of the scissors and thread is observed bending over his "mess"-table, whereon is spread a blanket, from which he quickly produces a unique garment known as the R. P. A. [Richmond Prison Association] style. In one day the cloth is cut, the body fitted, and the garment on. Who can imagine the pride felt by the wearer as he paces up and down "our promenade"? What cares he for blockades in time of war, for high tariffs in time of peace? Is he not the living emblem of the energy and skill of home manufacture?

36 *Union boy-soldier Simeon Bolivar Hulbert of Westfield, New York, was captured by five Alabamians near Richmond in 1862. He was first held in the Tobacco Warehouse Prison but was soon sent to Salisbury, where prisoners were confined in an old cotton factory. From there he was shipped to Belle Isle, where, he writes, there were five thousand prisoners on three acres of land. He arrived at Andersonville at the end of May 1864; all, he thought, would be safe if he minded his own business. He had an infection from an old arm wound, and though he did receive some medical care and remained optimistic about his recovery, he died of that and of diarrhea. The last entry in his diary is August 11, 1864.*

The following entries were made at Salisbury.

3 July 1862. In my bunk most all day. Have an extra dish today. Potter got three black Berry pies & we ate two of them. Keep the last one for the 4th July.

Funeral of a Lieut. today. Four men died last night in the hospital. The Lieut's remains were followed to the gate by a procession of soldiers or prisoners. The officers follow next to the coffin & the privates fall in the rear. Soon as we got to the gate the corpse was put into the waggon and drove through the gate & it closed upon us & he went out of our sight, we saw his remains no more.

4 July 1862. Great day for America. Speeches by several men in our prison & songs—America, that good tune, Red, White & Blue, Beautiful Flag & C.P.M. Officers amuse the prisoners— various amusement such as running with a wheelbarrow as fast as they can run & see how near they can come to a stake stuck in the ground. Grease a pig & then he that would ketch him by the tail has the pig. One of the privates caught him & so had the prize pig worth about three dollars. But here we are prisoners of war.

5 July 1862. Warm and pleasant. Wash my shirt to day. I have had to be my own wash woman now for six months past. Hope I shall be soon where I shall have my own mother & sisters to wash for me.

Get some Black Berries to day to eat. They are quite a relish though they are more sour than the berries in York State—they are very sour.

But now I should like to be at home & see my mother & sisters, father & Brothers. Get them to make me some nice Black Berry pies. They will beat the Southern women making pies, I tell you—these women are poor cooks!

37   *Howard C. Wright was brought up in the North, but as a young man he moved to New Orleans and became a happy and loyal southerner; he nevertheless retained strong family ties. When the Civil War broke out he joined the Louisiana Zouaves. From their encampment*

before Fort Pickens he wrote to his mother: "You know that my heart is with the cause of Southern rights and Southern independence and I am sure you cannot blame me for acting up to my conviction of right. I do not forget either that you are a South Carolinian. No one could regret a fratricidal war greater than myself but the South wanted peaceful secession and it was in the power of the dominant party of the North to arrange a happy division or by refusing it to plunge the country into a bloody war. They have chosen the latter."

Wright was captured at the Battle of Baton Rouge in 1863. He lived comfortably in New Orleans on parole for a few months and then was sent to Johnson's Island, Ohio. Exchanged in February 1865, he wrote again to his mother: "It is deplorable that a gulf of principle keeps me from your arms but it is there, and I would not, could not cross it." He was killed at West Point, Georgia, on April 14, 1865.

The letters below, written to an intimate family friend and to his sister, illustrate the continuing tension between family and conviction that Wright and many other Americans suffered during the war.

New Orleans, Oct 1, 1863

Henry A. Patterson

Dear Sir: I have just been notified to be in readiness to go off with about 150 other C.S. officers, prisoners of war, on the steamer Morning Star to New York. I do not know where we will be sent, but it will probably be where the other Port Hudson officers were sent to, who went on about two weeks ago, if you know where that is.

I write this to go off on a steamer this afternoon so that my family, through you, may know of it in advance, and for the especial object of getting you or sister Eleanor to induce mother not to make any attempts to visit me in prison. My reasons for not wishing any of my family to make this attempt are for their sake, not mine, of course, & can better be understood by you than by them. I can understand the feeling in the North toward "rebels" & the odium which might be cast upon anyone who even appeared to affiliate with them, while at the same time it would be no real gratification to any of my family to see me for a mere brief interval and as a prisoner. If mother cannot be content without seeing me it would be better to get me paroled for a few days, when I could come out in citizen's dress and see her & my sisters without the public display which would attend upon her visiting me. But I do not wish any application made to the authorities in my behalf by any of my family if it can be avoided. I can write to them (my family) from my prison, wherever it may be.

I have written to *you* because Eleanor may not be in the city and mother might see my name announced in the list of arrivals and take some step toward seeing me which might injure her in some way in the eyes of her Northern friends.

I am in excellent health and good spirits, confident of a speedy exchange and firm in the conviction of the righteousness of my cause. I have been treated with remarkable courtesy by the U.S. officers & expect to receive similar treatment while in their custody north. I need no clothing nor anything else whatever. I have been at perfect liberty for two months in this city and am merely notified now to come down aboard the steamer at the proper time, as if I were an invited guest instead of a prisoner of war.

Please give my love to sister Eleanor, Leeley, Bayard, Turner & all the juveniles & to mother & Hannah when you may see them.

Gratefully & Affectionately,

Governor's Island, Tuesday
1 o'clock PM

Dear Sir: If you see or have a chance to communicate with mother, my sisters or Charley please tell them that the reason I did not write from this place was the uncertainty of my position as well as the difficulty of communicating. I have received nothing in the way of news concerning my family since I have been here, which I attribute to the very strict regulations of the Department. The families of three officers have visited them on this island but I suppose they had some political influence. We are on the eve of departure for Johnson's Island. I will write after getting there. Give my love to all when you have a chance.

Affectionately

Johnson's Island, Ohio, Nov. 28, 1863

My dear sister Eleanor: Seeing ice on the ground this morning suggested the idea of using a pair of skates. It would be a good idea, if the Lake should freeze over this winter to start out bright and early some morning and skate over to Mr. Vallandigham's "cool retreat." Whether my host would agree to part with my agreeable company, however, is a question. Speaking of the impossibility of escape from this place I told Phoebe to send me a compressed india-rubber baloon & a copy of the N.Y. Herald with which to inflate it. On second thought, however, I think I would prefer the skates. The only way I could get them, however, would be for you to smuggle them to me in a paper of needles. Let's wait, though, and see what the Commissioners are going to do first. The U.S. Govt. have such a high opinion of my military abilities they don't want to exchange me, I know, but I think they will overcome their scruples before Spring. And although I will feel badly enough to be again out of communication with you for an indefinite period, still I will return to my country & my cause with the consciousness (whether in error or not) of doing my duty even at a sacrifice not merely of my own feelings of affection toward you all but of those of my mother and loving sisters. The contents of your letter of the 15th are all noted & the correction regarding the expressage of Nannie's box (so like you to make it, my ever conscientious Zellie) is all right. I am still in good health & spirits, living very nearly as comfortably & certainly without the cares & anxieties which wear down the scrupulous & faithful mother of a large family. Love to Henry, Leeley, Bayard & Turner & kisses to the chickens. Your affectionate brother.

Howard C. Wright Lt C.S.A.

38   *A tour de force of woodcarving, this chain with four fobs was made from one piece of wood by a Union soldier in the Andersonville, Georgia, stockade in 1864. Its intricacy and fine finish is characteristic of work by prisoners who have long, empty days to fill.*

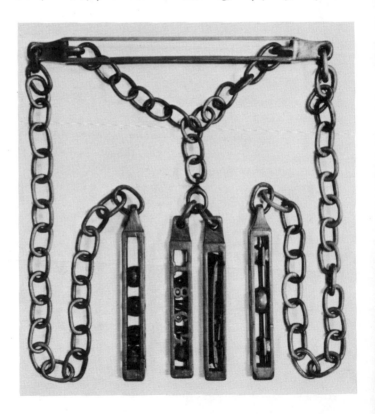

39 *Catherine Virginia Baxley was a Confederate blockade runner. Captured and imprisoned in 1862, she protested to the secretary of state that her travels were of an innocent, social nature: "Sir, Simply to gratify what I considered a pardonable curiosity—the desire to see Jeff. Davis—I undertook the now difficult and dangerous trip to Virginia by what I am told you are pleased to term the 'underground railway.' I carried with me nothing in the world but a few friendly letters packed it is true in my bonnet. I was not trusted with state papers. I am not fitted to be, being very nervous, impulsive and frank; in other words I never calculate." She was released beyond the Union lines after having signed a parole oath and went back to work for the "Cause," although she had sworn not to do so.*

On February 14, 1865, she was again a tenant of the Old Capitol Prison in Washington (so named because, after the burning of Washington by the British during the War of 1812, the building had been used to house the government). On that Valentine's Day the post commandant gave her a copy of Tennyson's Enoch Arden. *She used the margins, the interlines and the blank pages for the outpourings of her heart. Mrs. Surratt, described in the first entry, was tried and executed for complicity in the assassination of President Lincoln.*

Old Capitol Prison April 18, 1865. The 24 of this month shall have been here 3 months—*Tempis fugit.* The prison is filling up. Tonight we have Mrs. Surratt (how I envy this woman her cool calm self possession). I am equal to any emergency have any amount of energy but am too hot too hasty. All Mrs. S. lacks is judgment—there she is deficient. Her daughter Annie is with her, her niece & a Mrs. Fitzpatrick. Another arrival, a poor old lady verging upon her three score years; her crime—shaking a pair of Rebel breeches from the window and permitting the violin to be played in her house the day after Mr. Lincoln's death. Still another, Col. Thom. Green and lady, "no charges." And still another—a poor ignorant creature, who can neither read or write, her offense—charged with beating upon a *tin pan*

and singing rebel songs. . . . Another comes, poor old Mr.
Adams and wife, the keeper of a small wayside house in St.
Mary's chargd Booth stopped there and got a drink of water—
Comes a mulatrice and her son but "what has she done; the
presumption is she does not come under the head of the *Elect*
being a shade too light;" poor thing, she is unfortunate—some
Yankee parson or tutor visited her mother's neighborhood before
she was born. . . .

About 5 or half past five o'clock April 5 cannot sleep, get up
and sit with my face pressed against my bars in a little while
perceive an ambulance train winding round the south east
corner of the Capitol; passes in front of my windows. I perceive
the Gray Uniforms so dear to my heart—poor wounded Rebels
& Prisoners, God pity you. I kiss my hand to one, two, the
third ambulance is approaching. Two bodies on stretchers. I see
a pair of clasped hands raised toward me, a voice calls "Alls lost,
our Cause is hopeless and I am badly wounded." I am to
nearsighted to recognize the features and turn from the window.
half broken hearted, little dreaming it is my own and only child.
In a couple of hours the *Assist. Supt.* who is a *brute* in half
human form comes in to my room and in the most brutal &
unceremonious manner informs me my son is wounded and a
prisoner at the Lower or Old Capitol prison. God help me now,
my only child. I beg, I plead, implore to be taken to him. I
have [not] seen my child for two years—he is but a child. . . .
Tyranny again commences. I am not allowed to see my child, a
door only at the foot of the stairs separates us. I beg to be
allowed to call through the door and ask him how he is. "Don't
grieve *Ma* I am better." The excitement attendant upon Mr.
Lincoln's death affects him seriously, they repeat carelessly in his
presence the threats of the mob to tear the prison down and
murder the prisoners. On Saturday he has a hemorhage, on the
day of the procession he has a congestive chill—daily he grows
worse. I know my child's days, nay his very hours, are
numbered. Friday night, April 22, my darling beautiful boy

leaves me *all alone*. A few minutes before his death he asked me, "Ma is this my birthday"; again, "Kiss me Ma, like you used to when I was a little fellow and hold my hand Ma while I sleep"—a sleep from which only the trump of the Arch Angel will awake him. Why why am I so persecuted, what have I done more than others.

June 22d. Have just ordered the Yank at my door to stop fingering the key. I am quite well aware he is there and has me under lock and key without being constantly reminded of the fact by his play with the key.

40　*When Captain Henry Wirz, superintendent of the Confederate stockade at Andersonville, Georgia, was brought north to be tried for maliciously causing the suffering and death of thousands of Union prisoners of war, he was forced to wear a disguise so that he would not be mobbed by hate-filled Unionists. In Washington, he was incarcerated in the Old Capitol Prison. He said that he was offered his freedom if he would implicate Jefferson Davis, former president of the Confederacy, but he refused to do so. He was found guilty, hanged, and, denied consecrated ground, buried alongside those executed for the assassination of President Lincoln.*

Old Capitol Prison, Oct. 1, 1865
Everything is quiet around me. No sound but the measured steps of the sentinel in the corridor can be heard. The man who is sitting in my room is nodding in his chair. Poor, short-sighted mortals that we all are! This man is here to watch me, to prevent any attempt I might make to take my own life. My life —what is it worth to anyone except myself and my poor family, that they should be so anxious? I think I understand it very

well, they are afraid I might cheat them and the public at large from having their revenge, and giving, at the same time, the masses the benefit of seeing a man hanged. If this is all, they are welcome. I have no desire to live; perhaps there never was a more willing victim dragged to the scaffold than I am. Why should I desire to live? A beggar, crippled, and with my health and spirit broken—why oh why, should I desire to live? For the sake of my family? My family will do as well without me as with me. Instead of providing for and taking care of them, I would be a burden to them. And still, knowing all that, why do I not put an end to my life? Because, in the first instance, what I suffer now is the Will of God. GOD—how much is not in this word—what a tower of strength, of consolation! Yes, Heavenly Father, if it was not Thy will I would not be a prisoner. I would not be looked at, spoken of as a monster, such as the world has never seen and never will see. If that what I suffer now was not put on me by you for some wise purpose I would be as free as the bird in the air. Thou and I—we two alone know that I am innocent of those terrible charges. Thou and I—we both know that I never took the life of a fellow man —that I never caused a man to suffer and die in consequence of ill-treatment inflicted by me; and still I am tried for murder. Men have sworn that they saw me do it; they have called on Thee to witness that they would tell the truth, and still they told a lie—a lie as black as hell itself. Why did you not send a thunderbolt from the high heavens—why, oh God, why? Because it is Thy holy will, and in humility I kiss the rod with which Thou seest proper to chastise me.

The second reason why I did not destroy a life which is a burden to me, is because I owed it to myself, my family, my relatives, even to the world at large, to prove that there never existed a man so utterly devoid of all humanity, such a fiend incarnate, as it has been attempted to prove me to be. I see very well that I have no earthly show—that I am a doomed man; but thanks be to God that I am enabled to say with holy Stephanus: Lord, lay not this sin to their charge. They judge from what they hear and I must abide by it.

41 *Of Sing Sing in 1866, the Prison Association of New York reported: "Your committee were unable to ascertain the exact number of convicts who had served in the late war, but there is strong reason to believe that the great increase in the number now in confinement is due in no small degree to the circumstances of life and the depraved habits derived from the spirit of war." In August there was a revolt by inmates armed with stones, chunks of iron, and knives. It was quelled in half an hour, but only after one convict was killed, one escaped, and one guard was bruised.*

Reformers were searching for a gentler mode of government "in the prison for males, with slow, and cautious, and timid steps, and of course with only partial success; in the prison for females with bolder and more rapid strides, and with the happiest results," although it was very overcrowded, as Sing Sing was the only female prison for felons in New York State. There were, in many cases two women to a cell.

Addie Irving's letters present a glimpse of life there. The indomitable and wiley Addie was a recidivist; jobs for all women, but especially for ex-convicts, were hard to find. She kept bad company and stole when she could. She once escaped from Blackwell's with the agent's son, whom she says she later married. But he went away to war and she was on her own and in trouble soon again. While she was at Mount Pleasant (Sing Sing) she was visited by the charitable Mrs. E. C. Buchanan of 24 East 33rd Street, New York; she is the "Beloved lady" to whom these cheerfully fawning letters were addressed. They were also undoubtedly intended for the Matron, who would have censored them.

Beloved Lady,

I received a letter from you the Oct. 14th dated September 21st. I cannot think where the delay has been. Mrs. H. says it only came Saturday. How gentle lady can i thank you for your kind solicitude toward *me* whom the nearest of kindred have forsaken? Oh! Mrs. B. I can hardly frame words to express my gratitude. Yes as you write I have great cause to thank God for his mercy to me in giving me such a friend to love. I think I would be the happiest person in this world to have you for my friend, my guide, my councillor, when I leave this "House of Reproach," here you seem to think that I am safe! Oh! you little know how many the temptations are which surround me here. It is verry hard to listen to the falsehoods some of these creatures will tell to try & injure those who try to do right. It is good to have Dear Mrs. Hubbard. She has a verry trying place, a great deal of care, but manages with admirable patience all her affairs. You sent me some pens. Mrs. H. forgot to give them to me till she saw them mentioned in your letter (she has so much to attend to. you have to expect she cannot do every thing at once) they are verry good. indeed i rather prefer Gilletts pens. Mrs. H. gave me a present of a Common prayer Book. i read it every day & night. I feared Dear Lady that you were offended with me for being so familiar (asking for your picture) but i could not resist I feel as *you*—"we know not what a day may bring forth" I feel if i had your dear face to look upon it would keep me in the right way. (your image is indelibly stamped on my heart. Yet, to obtain a minature of you i would do almost any thing) I often picture up to myself a pair of dark love light eyes looking down in pity & sympathy on me, a dear little mouth with the sweetest expression saying "not the righteous, sinners Jesus came to call" and darling little curls framing that altogether angelical countenance is it not a correct picture? please let me know the age of your little ones. If you

80

send me some tidy cotton (in a little box care of Mrs. H.) i will make you some Handsome tidies. please send a couple of spools 20 thread I will make lace trimming for the little ones (I want to send them a nice gift on thanksgiving.) Send a little pink tidy cotton too if you have any little Scraps of silk I would like them to make some fancy articles for you. enclosed you will find a little collar I could make it a great deal nicer only it might be to heavy. That blank book will be just the thing i need I am certainly ashamed of my pen*manship* I have neglected my writing shamefully and I thank you exceedingly for your proffered kindness—to improve me I can imbroidcr beautifully but my sight is so poor at present I do not sew at all. The Dr. said ear rings would be verry good for my eyes if you have a small pair you can spare i may Reciprocate the favor. if you would be so kind as to send them to me I have all thoes little papers. since Jan. God has dealt verry mercifull with us here there has been no severe cases of sickness here since my incarceration (15 months) We had some quaker Ladies hold a meeting here some time ago, when the inmates (all with the exception of thoes who were at work) attended. Our Chaplain Rev. J. B. Smith has been absent for some time. during his absence the village pastor assumed hs duties in trying to turn this preverse people in the straight & narrow way. The rules are verry easy to be obeyed the matrons good & kind. Mrs. H. at their head sees that the matron's do justice to the inmates. as well as she commands Respect & obedience from the Prisoners to thoes in charge God bless you & strengthen you in your labour.

To bring the erring ones to Christ is the prayer of your grateful

Addie

In a biographical letter Addie Irving relates a troubling experience that occurred at the prison on Blackwell's Island. It was not an

*unusual one as is evident from this appraisal of women's fate in city
penal institutions in 1845: "So free is the intercourse among the
inmates of those prisons and so effectually is the contamination of
evil communication encouraged, nay, insured and enforced by the
manner in which they are organized; that it is to us a matter of great
doubt, whether it would not be better for an innocent female to be
consigned at once to a brothel than to be confined in either of those
prisons. In the former case, she would at least enjoy the advantage
of being able to fly from the approach of corruption at her pleasure."
Similar conditions are deplored throughout prison literature.*

One evening about 9 o'clock most of the prisoners were asleep.
Mr. Keen the Warden came down to the prison accompanied
by a navy officer he called for me and said "Addie here is a
gentleman your mother sent to you" then turning to the gent
he said "she is not naturally wayward only a love of mischief
&c" the commodore asked him if he could see me in private.
Mr. Keen told him to take me into the Reception Room: When
we went in there he turned and Bolted the door (I had 2
brothers in the navy & I feared lest I should hear ill news of
them) I said Oh Sir tell me quickly what you have to say he
turned and said. you know what i am here for & tried to kiss
me. he told me my mother did not ever see him. But if I
submitted to him he would give me a ladies life and I need
never steal again he would have me pardoned and gratify my
least wish. God was watching over me then and gave me
strength. I gained the victory & foiled the villain! he had the
effrontery to tell me to call aloud if I was so disposed that the
authorities sent him there. I did not lest i should shame Mr.
Keen's wife whoes gentleness won my love. I had witness to
this, the old keeper who unlocked my cell is dead, George
Arculariens. Another keeper who saw the introduction and heard
the conversation is still on the island, Phillip Brown. Now I ask

you after being in such a contaminating place is it any wonder i yealded to temptation again.

42 *Justice was swift in the western boom towns during and after the Civil War, and it was often extralegal; for it became customary for vigilante committees to assume the powers that duly constituted officials failed to exercise either because they were unwilling or unable to do so. In the summer of 1864 in the Montana Territory, James Brady shot one Murphy with whom he had been feuding for some time, but he did not kill him. Brady was soon ferreted out of the Beaver Head Saloon in Virginia City by a posse of twelve vigilantes; he was found guilty the following morning and executed that afternoon. It is reported that two hundred armed men escorted him to his execution and that five thousand people assembled to witness it. To save time and money, a butcher's hoist was used as a gallows, a box and a plank rigged for the drop. His last words to the world were that it was the first action of the kind that he had done, that he was intoxicated and insane, and that he hoped his execution would be a warning to others. He was then launched into eternity. He left this letter for his daughter.*

My Dear Daughter: You will never see me again. In an evil hour, being under the control and influence of whiskey, I tried to take the life of my fellow-man. I tried to shoot him through a window. He will in all probability die—and that at my hands. I cannot say that I should not suffer the penalty affixed to the violation of the law. I have been arrested, tried and sentenced to be hanged by the Vigilance Committee. In one short hour I will have gone to eternity. It is an awful thought; but it is my own fault. By the love I feel for you, in this, my dying hour, I entreat you to be a good girl. Walk in the ways of the Lord. Keep Heaven, God and the interest of your soul, before your eyes. I commend and commit you to the keeping of God. Pray for my soul. Farewell, forever.

Your father,
James Brady

L. H. Musgrove was the leader of an organized network of horse-thieves, highwaymen, and murderers whose territory included Colorado, New Mexico, Wyoming, Nebraska, and Kansas. In 1867–1868 its headquarters were in Denver, Colorado Territory. Musgrove was finally caught and hanged by vigilantes composed of the town's most esteemed doctors, lawyers, and businessmen, in their words, "by the people and for the people." One official did try to lecture the crowd on the illegality of the proceedings, but even Musgrove was not impressed; standing on his wagon scaffold with the noose around his neck, he simply rolled and smoked his last cigarette.

Before his execution he wrote these farewell letters.

Denver November 23d, 1868

My Dear Brother

I am to be hung to-day on false charges by a mob my children is in Napa Valley Cal—will you go and get them & take caree of them for me godd Knows that I am innocent pray for me but I was here when the mob took me. Brother good by for Ever take care of my pore little children I remain your unfortunate Brother

good by
L. H. Musgrove

Denver, C.T.

My Dear Wife—before this reaches you I will be no more Mary I am as you know innocent of the charges made against

me I do not know what they are agoing to hang me for unless
it is because I am acquainted with Ed Franklin—godd will
protect you hope Good by for ever yours sell what I have and
keep it.

L. H. Musgrove

*L. P. Griswold was a judge for the vigilantes; he would kill a man
for a few dollars, then rob him; or he would rob someone else and
report the lynched man as the culprit. When he was killed trying to
escape from jail, General D. J. Cook, chief of the Rocky Mountain
Detective Association, is reported to have said: "Old Griswold was
a curse to all who came in contact with him. He did not die any too
soon, and the world would have probably been better had he never
been born." This is a letter, translated from cipher, to his common-
law wife, developing a plot for escape from jail. Fear of similar
messages is still used to justify rigorous prison mail censorship.*

Dear Jennie—The horses must not be more than two blocks
away; we will come out of the front door, and you or Alex—
ought to be on the opposite side of the street, so that when we
went out you could walk by where the horses were, and then
there could be no mistake. We only want the horses now to go
to the mountains. I want Alex to come and get them. Then you
or him see Henry and have other ones got. I do not know
whether we will have Spencers or Winchesters; we will have one
or the other, but we may not get cartridges. Have Alex get 5
hundred rounds of each, so we can take which ever we want;
also twenty-five rounds of 36, and the same of 44. Those we
don't want he can take back. Have plenty of cakes. Take two
sacks, a part full of eatables; they must be more than half full,
so that we can lay them across the saddles, one sack on each
horse. The principal things are bread; hard tack if you can get
it; no more than seven or eight pounds of bacon; lots of salt and

pepper, and lots of coffee, ground. Mind you, lots of that is all that has kept me alive. You had better have a quart of whiskey on each saddle, for we are nothing but skin and bones, and very weak. We can not ride far without stimulants. We will stay near Denver until we get strength; we are getting worse every day, and I assure you I will not leave here until I square accounts with Smith. . . . Better get some chewing tobacco. I want one bottle of morphine, for riding will hurt me. . . .

On Griswold's dead body were found two leaves from Harper's *magazine containing the poem "Hannah Jane" and a scrap of paper with the following conundrum in cipher.*

A problem: A prisoner anxious to escape, and a dead man awaiting burial; how were these two things to be exchanged so that the living man might pass out without going to the grave.

III

The first National Congress on Penitentiary and Reformatory Discipline met in Cincinnati, Ohio, on October 12, 1870, "for the promotion of the welfare and reformation of unfortunate humanity." The temporary chairman, Major A. T. Goshorn, summed up the task at hand in his welcoming address.

"The object of your coming together is one which should engage the sympathy and cooperation of all good citizens throughout the land. With a rapidly increasing population and the disposition of the people to congregate in large cities, we have an alarming increase of crime, and legislation is obliged to be ever devising new remedies and imposing fresh penalties for the protection of society. But while our civilization is marked by its advanced and prompt legislation and distinguished for its physical care of criminals, prison discipline and the reformation of the convict are still an unsolved problem, notwithstanding their high importance in establishing public security and social harmony. It is not enough that we erect great prison-houses, grand in conception, beautiful in architectural design and finish, and liberal in their appointments. These are monuments of the prosperity of the state and evidences of the determination of society to protect itself against evil-doers; but the granite walls and iron-bars, although they deprive the criminal of his liberty and inflict a just physical punishment, do not work that reformation in the soul of the man, that will restore him to society regenerated and reformed. Until this is in some measure accomplished, our system of prison discipline is imperfect and ineffectual.

"It is never to be forgotten that the criminal is a man, and entitled to all the offices of humanity, which are consistent with the treatment of him as a criminal. That humanitarian sentiment which would reject all punishment is inconsistent with the proper control of the vicious passions and desires of men, and would quickly demoralize society, and subvert the very foundations of moral and civil government.

"The dignity of the law must be vindicated, and society must be protected by the prompt and decisive punishment of crime. It cannot be otherwise in a well constituted goverment. . . ."

43 *Delay in the judicial process resulting in prolonged pretrial confinement is not a phenomenon of modern times, nor is the state's hope than an arrestee will provide evidence leading to the conviction of others.*

Moyamensing Prison Feb. 25th 71

To His Honor Judge Cadwalader

Dear Sir—Having been incarcerated Here Since the 31st of August now nearly six months I would like to either have trial or discharge. The facts pertaining to the cause of my arrest And imprisonmint are simply as follows: Last August I collected Some money Due me from diffrent parties Among which was a ten dollar not counterfeit, which i Paid to the Landlord for my Bill not knowing At the time its being counterfeit. But as Soon as it was Discovered to Be Bad i redeemed it and destroyed it that is tare it up as i did not know from whom I had received It to return it I have been visited By officials to make disclosures of others engaged in the business so that the ends of Justice might Be met but as i had never been In the business i could tell them nothing otherwise i should have done so, consequently i have been abandoned to my fate hoping that your Honor will favorably consider my case i remain

Your humble Servant
Henry C. Paul

44 *Seth Wilbur Payne expressed an unacceptable opinion in the* Utica Bee, *was tried and sentenced, and "Presto, sheared shaved redressed and caged. Thirty minutes ago I was breathing the free pure air of this bright afternoon. On my way hither I passed groups of happy children and beautifully dressed ladies. Never before had I so fully realized the blessings of freedom."*

Although "communicating with a fellow prisoner by sign word or writing was the greatest crime next to that of breaking jail," he found the following note in his cell. It had been penciled on eight bits of paper and hidden in his water cup. The time: March 23, 1873; place: Albany Prison, Cell 62. Payne never talked with its author, but had access to his cell as he was a tier sweeper.

MY DEAR POOR STUDENT:—I was truly glad to see you, but very sorry to have seen you in this deplorable situation. I can not imagine, for the life of me, what it could have been that sent you here. I really hope your stay is short. I have been here one year and have two and a half years yet to stay unless pardoned out. I trust you will forgive me for taking the unwarranted liberty of writing to you. Circumlocution or form is out of the question here. We have to be as laconic as possible and decorum is suspended "pro tem." Any time you may choose to write me, you can do so with perfect safety; you will find under the shelf in my cell, a secret shelf that you can put a note in for me; it will be known to no one, save you and I. You will also find a volume of Wood's Natural History in my cell which you can take at any time and peruse. Also, any other book, or anything else you may there find is at your liberty. Should I write you hereafter, you will find it on the aforesaid secret shelf. If you want a knife to use in your cell, you may take the one you will find on this shelf and keep it while you are here, but don't let any one see it. Are you acquainted with the editor of the Temperance Patriot at Utica? If you have no soap I will give you a piece. Is there any stirring news outside? What is the situation between the United States and Spain? How have the Alabama claims been settled? I, of course have not seen a paper or heard a word of news since I was sentenced a year ago. If you have plenty of pencil I should be extremely obliged to you for a small piece as mine is quite finished. I am an artist by profession, and am here for defrauding the U.S.

Mail Department. Enclosed you will find my grandfather's address; if you should go before me, please do me the favor to write to him. With best wishes for your welfare and comfort, I am most respectfully, yours,

HAMLIN

P.S.—My cell is 163.

45   *"Good many. Kiowas, Comanches, and Arapahows, Cheyenne all together with soldiers and Capt. Pratt take us to Florida. . . . After a while Capt. Pratt took off all Indian chains, but not too quick. . . . By and by teacher she come with pictures of dog, cat, cow and tell us every day nine o'clock morning we go to school stop twelve o'clock. . . . Before Indians went to school, Capt. Pratt he gave Indians clothes just like white men, but Indians no want hair cut. . . ." So spoke Cheyenne warrior Bears Heart of his incarceration at Fort Marion. While in prison Bears Heart made many spirited pictures. The drawing on the following page is from a group done in 1876, which depict the stages of the month-long trip east from Fort Sill and various aspects of life at Fort Marion. The title was supplied by Captain Pratt.*

46   *William Marcy ("Boss") Tweed was the head of the ring that robbed the City of New York of countless millions of dollars in the early 1870s. Arrested and found guilty on two hundred and four of two hundred and twenty counts in 1874, he was sentenced to twelve years' imprisonment and a twelve-thousand-dollar fine, but he was released after having served only one year on Blackwell's Island. The state then arrested him for a debt of six million dollars; bail was fixed at three million dollars. As he was unable to pay and his friends were*

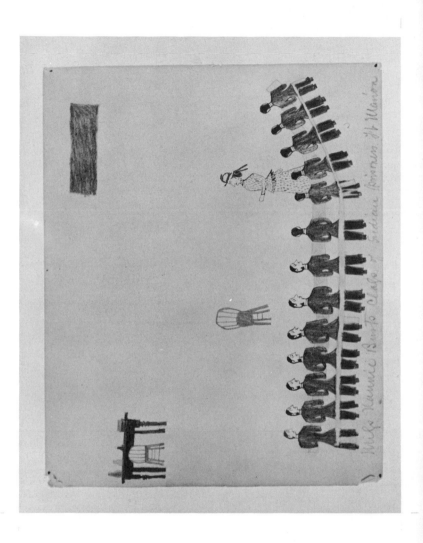

unwilling to endanger themselves by coming forward to help him, he was sent to the debtors' prison on Ludlow Street. There he paid seventy-five dollars a week to the jailer for two spacious rooms handsomely decorated to his personal taste with etchings, geraniums, and overstuffed chairs. He rode out in his carriage every day, dined at home, and escaped. Disguised, he successfully reached St. Augustine, Florida, and Santiago, Cuba. Then he attempted to flee to Spain; although he was scrubbing the decks dressed as a common sailor when the brig landed, he was recognized by Spanish officials and returned to the United States.

It is said that the offer he made to inform in the following letter was turned down because Governor Samuel Tilden, for political reasons, wished to limit prosecution of the ring solely to Tweed.

Ludlow Street Jail
New York, Dec. 5th, 1876

Charles O'Connor, Esq.

Sir: I take the liberty of addressing you this letter in view of the fact that your position as counsel for the State authorities is professed solely for the public good regardless of any factions or personal interest.

Heretofore I have responded in the courts and met my troubles with every resource at my disposal. *Possibly* in the mistaken sense of duty I have stood up too long to shield others as well as myself, bearing such losses and punishments as were meted out to me in my misfortunes, and it was truly in the interests of others, more than in my own, that litigations and resistances were prolonged. . . .

I am an old man, greatly broken in health, and cut down in spirits and can no longer bear my burden, and to mitigate the prospects of hopeless imprisonment, which must speedily terminate my life, I should, it seems to me, make any sacrifice or effort. . . . I would not make this futile offer if I had not had some assurance through your published statements that the

vindication of principle and the prospect of permanently
purifying the public service was the object you have in view as
being more desirable than the recovery of money. If in any
manner you see fit to use me for such purposes, I shall be only
too glad to respond, trusting implicitly in your high reputation
and character. . . . I hope to have any matters affecting other
persons restricted to your *personal* knowledge and discretion.
Knowing as you do every material fact already it would be
unavailing for me to withhold any details you may demand. I
only ask in qualification that your more reliable judgment shall
take the responsibility of publication and the use of such
matters only as may be necessary for the ends you may wish to
advance. For the present I have no legal counsel. I shall not
employ any except to aid in the spirit of this communication,
and conform to the usages of the courts. . . .

Very truly yours,
William M. Tweed

47 *The temptation to regard convicts as a cheap source of state labor
has always been hard to resist, especially by transportation officials.
E. C. Wines in his comprehensive work* The State of Prisons and
of Child-Saving Institutions in the Civilized World, *published in
1880, describes the penal situation in North Carolina as follows:*

*"At this time there would seem to be a rivalry of the several
sections of the State to send as many convicts as possible to the
penitentiary. Railroads are building, and other improvements going
on all over the State, and it is now the policy of the legislature to grant
convict labor in aid of these works. It follows that the greater the
number of convicts the larger the grants; the greater the number of
such works undertaken the more rapidly they can be completed. This
dispersion of the convict labor over the State makes it impossible to
effect any thing, even though desired, towards their instruction or
reformation. It like-wise exposes them to being overworked and to*

cruel treatment. They are exposed to a strong temptation to escape. Whenever this is attempted they are shot down like dogs. During the years 1877–78 twelve men were thus killed."

Five hundred convicts laid the rails into the mountain fastness of Asheville, North Carolina; the track doubled and redoubled to make eight almost complete circles and there were multiple tunnels cut through solid granite, the longest being eighteen thousand feet at Swannanoa. Over two and a half thousand citizens cheered the first train as it pulled into Asheville on October 3, 1880. The photograph was taken as an advertising card for Lindsey's Photographic Parlors, Couth Court Place, Asheville, North Carolina.

48 Cole Younger began his career as an outlaw in the troubled borderlands of Missouri and Kansas during the Civil War. Incensed that the Kansas militia had devastated his father's and his neighbors' farms, he joined Quantrell in a guerrilla gang that fought for the South and for freedom; he was commissioned in the Confederate army in 1865. After the war he and three of his brothers joined Frank and Jesse James in a series of spectacular bank robberies. They were notoriously successful. Then in 1874 during the Northfield Bank robbery, Cole and his two remaining brothers, riddled with bullets, were caught and brought to justice. Imprisoned for life in the Stillwater, Minnesota, penitentiary, Cole studied theology, Jim, law, and Bob, medicine. They had adjoining cells, but could converse with each other officially only once a month.

The letters below are from Cole to a persistent, would-be biographer who also had an interest in religious subjects.

Stillwater, Minn, Oct 20, 1880

J. W. Buel, Esq.

Dear Sir: Your letter was received some days ago. The reason I did not answer soon was owing to the fact that when we were first captured, I received a great many letters from different parties all wanting to write a history of my life, and to be just to all I replied to none. But as yours is the only letter of the kind I have received for a long time, I have concluded to write you.

Without intending the least disrespect, permit me to say: Positively, I will have nothing to do with writing a history of any kind. Now if you have determined to prepare such a history —and I presume you have—I will aid you only so much as to refer you to those who served with me in the Lost Cause. You will find the names of all of them in Edwards' book, entitled "Shelby and his Men". Most of these men still live in Jackson, Cass, Johnson and Lafayette counties; I am willing to abide by any statement they may make concerning me.

As for anything since the war, a true statement would fall flat. I am aware that my name has been connected with all the bank robberies in the country; but positively I had nothing to do with any one of them. I look upon my life since the war as a blank, and will never say anything to make it appear otherwise. *The world may believe as it pleases.*

I presume that you are a professional writer, and, like many others, have been led to believe by sensational newspaper reports, that there are historical facts sufficient connected with my life to make an interesting book, but it is a mistake, unless nine-tenths of the matter is fiction. . . .

Very respectfully,
T. C. Younger

In a letter of October 31, 1880, Cole detailed his position further.

. . . You announce your desire to question me concerning the James Boys. Of course I have no idea of the nature of your questions, but if they involve information respecting what they have been accused of since the war, then I will make no answer.

If either of them ever trusted me with a secret, there is no power on earth that could induce me to betray that trust—nor that of any one else. No matter how much I might condemn the act, or how bitter enemies we might have become afterward, it would be all the same. . . .

There is one thing I wish you would note respecting the character of the guerillas. It is the popular impression among people of other States that we were sneak-thieves like the bushwhackers of Virginia, Tennessee and Arkansas, who hid in the mountains and sallied out during the night to kill old men and rob defenseless women and children. This you know is a fallacy and an unjust stigma upon the guerillas.

. . . The only bulldozing I ever did was in making men who remained at home during the winter of '62 get wood for the women and children; for the wives of Union as well as Confederate soldiers.

The question has been asked thousands of times: "Why have the Youngers been protected and befriended so long by the people in the western counties of Missouri?" There are two reasons: First, because they never believed we were guilty of the crimes charged upon us; and second, because I befriended them during the war. At the most critical period of the great strife, in 1862, we had five different farms in Cass and Jackson counties, with corn cribs full of corn. When food became difficult to obtain, I told all the poor people to help themselves and take what corn they needed, without charge. . . . There are many mothers, wives and daughters still living who will credit me with an honorable part during the war, and of risking my life in the defense of their fathers, husbands and brothers. I never, in any circumstances, refused to aid a friend, regardless of political predilections, a claim which not one of my old comrades will dispute.

I have written you more than I intended when I commenced. I will ask you to pay no attention to what I have said, until all my assertions are corroborated by other sources, satisfactory to yourself; then use the facts as you deem proper.

I was a soldier and fought to hurt, but I never molested non-combatants.

T.C. Younger.

49 *Pedro Dominicus, a Mexican, was arrested in 1879 as a accomplice in the lynching of Luther Mitchell and Ami Ketchum, homesteaders in Custer County, Nebraska. Mitchell and Ketchum were, at the time, in custody for having shot a rich cattleman who had tried to drive them from their farm. In collusion with the sheriff, the cattleman's gang kidnaped the prisoners; their bodies were found in a canyon, hanged by ropes without slipknots, and brutally burned. Dominicus turned state's evidence and was given his freedom. While imprisoned during the trial, he braided the horsehair bridle and cinch, pictured on the next page, for the wife of the deputy sheriff who apprehended him.*

50 *The reports of John Purves, nightkeeper for thirty-four years in the Southern Michigan Prison at Jackson, were preserved when the old prison, built in 1839, was torn down and replaced by the present structure in 1926. They have run weekly in* The Spectator, *Jackson's inmate newspaper, and are reported to be the most widely reprinted feature in America's approximately one-hundred-and-ninety-member Penal Press. Here are some sample entries from the mid-1880s; the originals were penned in a careful Spenserian script.*

June 18—A new crank has entered into the rank of trouble makers. No. 2742, Schneider, who always has been quiet and

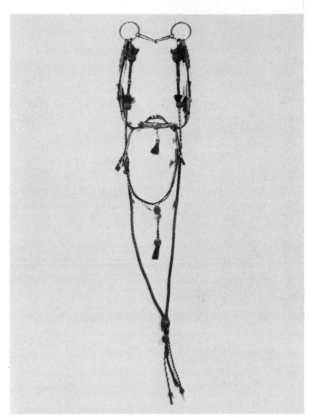

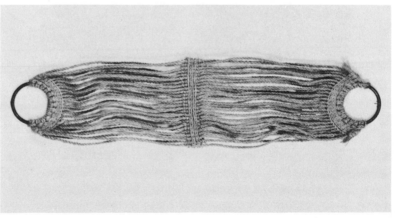

steady, suddenly went berserk in the dining room, throwing fish stew all over his neighbors and screaming at the top of his voice: "Hallelujah, the day has come." I cannot understand what has happened to this man.

June 19—The prison has been fairly quiet this night. The Chaplain attempted to talk with Schneider, but received nothing but foul abuse and strong words. It is my considered opinion that the rule prohibiting talking amongst the prisoners results in their minds breaking. Judicious selections of newspapers might serve to release this tension under which the convicts labor.

June 29—The convicts were noisy and restless throughout the night. An excessively hot and damp spell has brought about the complaints about bed bugs. I wish there was some sure way to rid the place of this pesky nuisance. Clancy, No. 2932, continues to irritate his cell-bound neighbors with that incessant hawking and rattling cough which he affects. I do not blame the men for complaining in this respect for he is a most bothersome convict, and unclean in person and habit, more so than any received here in many years. The solution to this type of problem, no doubt, lies in the establishment of a separate gallery for all such as he, but I should not relish the job of guarding it.

June 30—Fairly good order prevailed throughout the night, although it has been stifling hot. I ordered extra water passed around at eleven o'clock and the convicts seemed to appreciate this consideration. Clancy, No. 2932, continues to annoy his neighbors with that coughing and wheezing of his. It is reported that during the day, when no one is near his cell, never a sound comes from him and that he starts his irritating noise only when others are nearby. I moved him to a base cell near the guard desk where he can be watched more closely. The floor in the bathroom needs repairing. It's rotting away, and someday someone will crash through.

July 18—It was necessary for me to put the iron hat on Cook, No. 3129, this night for disobeying an order given him by the keeper. As a mild disciplinary measure, the iron hat may prove to be effective. The only difficulty I have encountered is the fitting of the basket-shaped contrivance over a refractory convict's head. As a suggestion, may I point out that perhaps the shaping of the iron strips to better fit the head of the convict might make a difference, and as the convict is to wear the iron hat day and night until the period of his punishment is over, a neater fit would eliminate such sores as occur from chafing caused by the constant wearing of the hat.

July 19—The night passed quietly barring the lamentable accident that happened to Keeper Rowan. Someone, and I am convinced that it was a convict, opened the main sewer cover in the basement. Rowan, walking in the darkness, stepped into it. The cover was in place at count time when I inspected the basement previously. All the guards on duty stoutly deny any knowledge of the circumstances. Rowan, was removed to the hospital down-town.

July 20—Muhlberg, No. 1092, was unable to attend school, having received ten licks with the leather strap during the afternoon for stealing leather from the contract shop. Was he excused by the doctor? Cary, Jumbo, and Brahm, all who have been on good behaviour for the past few nights have made up for lost time tonight by screaming and raising a rumpus in general. I warned them they would get the water treatment if they didn't stop their noise. Carey, No. 3113, had the insolence to yell, "Bring your old hose, I need a bath anyway." I opened the window first letting in the cold air, and one squirt from the force pump silenced him at once, and he begged to have the window closed again. I told him if he so much as lets out another peep this night I would keep the window wide open. He promised to remain quiet and he did, and that was that. I rather think he fears the cold night air more than anything else.

July 21—The low whistle was heard again by Baird. This time there was no wind blowing. A West Wing convict informs that there is a plot hatching to make a break on the walls. I ordered the entire wing to be searched but no contraband was found except three cigars which were stolen from the contract shop by Leslie, No. 1102. He is an old offender in this, and although punishment seems to do him no good, I chalked him in.

51 *The 1890s was marked by dramatic organized confrontations between labor and management. The Homestead Strike of the Amalgamated Association of Iron, Steel and Tin Workers against the Carnegie Steel Company over wage cuts was one of the most violent. When the state militia and scabs reopened the plant, only a small percentage of the original working force was rehired.*

Shortly after the strike was broken, Alexander Berkman, a Russian-born anarchist, shot and stabbed, but failed to kill, Carnegie's general manager, Henry Clay Frick. He was sentenced to twenty-one years' imprisonment in the Western Penitentiary of Pennsylvania at Pittsburgh. Released in thirteen years, he edited Mother Earth, *the anarchist monthly. He was deported from the United States in 1919, as a result of the November 7, 1919, government raid, directed by Attorney General A. Mitchell Palmer against known and suspected radicals.*

Berkman maintained an elaborate system for spiriting private correspondence beyond the walls. This letter recording his intense suffering was written after he had been in prison for five years.

Dear K.

I know you must have been worried about me. Give no credence to the reports you hear. I did not try to suicide. I was very nervous and excited over the things that happened while I was in the dungeon. I saw the papers after I came up—you know what they said. I couldn't sleep; I kept pacing the floor. The screws were hanging about my cell, but I paid no attention to them. They spoke to me, but I wouldn't answer: I was in no mood for talking. They must have thought something wrong with me. The doctor came, and felt my pulse, and they took me to the hospital. The Warden rushed in and ordered me into a strait-jacket. "For safety," he said.

You know Officer Erwin; he put the jacket on me. He's a pretty decent chap; I saw he hated to do it. But the evening screw is a rat. He called three times during the night, and every time he'd tighten the straps. I thought he'd cut my hands off; but I wouldn't cry for mercy, and that made him wild. They put me in the "full size" jacket that winds all around you, the arms folded. They laid me, tied in the canvas, on the bed, bound me to it feet and chest, with straps provided with padlocks. I was suffocating in the hot ward; could hardly breathe. In the morning they unbound me. My legs were paralyzed, and I could not stand up. The doctor ordered some medicine for me. The head nurse (he's in for murder, and he's rotten) taunted me with the "black bottle." Every time he passed my bed, he'd say "You still alive? Wait till I fix something up for you." I refused the medicine, and then they took me down to the dispensary, lashed me to a chair, and used the pump on me. You can imagine how I felt. That went on for a week; every night in the strait-jacket, every morning the pump. Now I am back in the block, in 6 A. A peculiar coincidence,—it's the same cell I occupied when I first came here.

Don't trust Bill Say. The warden told me he knew about the

note I sent you just before I smashed up. If you got it, Bill must have read it and told Sandy. Only dear old Horsethief can be relied upon.

How near the boundary of joy is misery! I shall never forget the first morning in the jacket. I passed a restless night, but just as it began to dawn I must have lost consciousness. Suddenly I awoke with the most exquisite music in my ears. It seemed to me as if the heavens had opened in a burst of ecstasy. . . . It was only a little sparrow, but never before in my life did I hear such sweet melody. I felt murder in my heart when the convict nurse drove the poor birdie from the window ledge.

A.

52 *Geronimo, war-shaman of the Chiricahua, a proud, aggressive Apache tribe whose ancestral lands lay in what is now southeastern Arizona, fought fiercely in every way he could devise against the encroachment of the whites on Apache territory and the impoverishing reservation way of life. Finally, in 1886, outnumbered by the whites, his followers decimated by cold, hunger, and despair, Geronimo surrendered. He was sent as a prisoner of war to Fort Marion in Florida. Later he was transferred to Fort Sill, Oklahoma, where, in 1905, he told the story of his life through a fellow warrior-interpreter to S. M. Barrett, superintendent of education in Lawton, Oklahoma. Although the manuscript failed to receive the approval of the U.S. War Department, it was neither censured nor denied publication.*

The Apache derives spiritual strength from a recitation of his earliest origins, and he continually relates to them. Thus Geronimo opens his life saga by narrating the Chiricahua creation myth, which climaxes with the advent of a being named Apache. In conclusion Geronimo comments:

We are vanishing from the earth, yet I cannot think we are useless or Usen would not have created us. He created all tribes of men and certainly had a righteous purpose in creating each.

For each tribe of men Usen created He also made a home. In the land created for any particular tribe He placed whatever would be best for the welfare of that tribe.

When Usen created the Apaches He also created their homes in the West. He gave them such grain, fruits, and game as they needed to eat. To restore their health when disease attacked them He made many different herbs to grow. He taught them where to find these herbs, and how to prepare them for medicine. He gave them a pleasant climate and all they needed for clothing and shelter was at hand.

Thus it was in the beginning: the Apaches and their homes each created for the other by Usen himself. When they are taken from these homes they sicken and die. How long will it be until it is said, there are no Apaches?

Geronimo spoke thus of Apache justice:

If an Apache had allowed his aged parents to suffer for food or shelter, if he had neglected or abused the sick, if he had profaned our religion, or had been unfaithful, he might be banished from the tribe.

The Apaches had no prison as white men have. Instead of sending their criminals into prison they sent them out of their tribe. These faithless, cruel, lazy, or cowardly members of the tribe were excluded in such a manner that they could not join any other tribe. Neither could they have any protection from our unwritten tribal laws. Frequently these outlaw Indians banded together and committed depredations which were charged against the regular tribe. However, the life of an outlaw Indian was a hard lot, and their bands never became very large;

besides, these bands frequently provoked the wrath of the tribe and secured their own destruction.

53 *The poems of James Gordon Stell, an inmate of the Iowa State Prison at Fort Madison, were first published under the aegis of the prison and later in an anthology by the Chautauqua Society, which hoped to whet popular interest in penal reform, and by proponents of the Lyceum Course in Prison, a form of educational entertainment. Before the collection went to print Stell wrote to the editor: "As you know, my case came up in April for action after several months of 'stalling.' I haven't a pen-scratch since then. Such delay fills the insane ward and you need not be surprised if I am among the future transferred. It is inevitable as I feel myself slipping mentally every day. Of course, I am fighting it, but each day brings some new fact of broken faith and unfairness that cannot be forgotten. I have been here over four years—a greater crime than I committed to come here! One thing is certain, I have made my last effort to get out because I know it is useless."*

A few weeks later Stell broke into the photography room and drank what he presumably thought was grain alcohol; it was denatured alcohol. When informed of his death, his relatives requested the warden to bury his body at the prison.

"Mourn Not for Me" is one of the few compositions that deal with the suffering of the families of prisoners.

Mourn Not for Me

Mourn not for me because my shame
Is hedged by towered walls,
And black across my humbled name
A hated number falls.

Weep for yourself, and not for me;
   Dear, all your flood of tears
Can never set the captive free
   Nor cleanse his sullied years.

You are the one who, night and morn
   And all the day between,
Must suffer most from venomed scorn,
   Most learn that men are mean.

When you have fled from wanton sneers
   To lonely haggard hours,
Then, if you mourn, let many tears
   Be for this world of ours—

This selfish world, that reads no score
   Of souls that writhed and died
Before the studded iron door
   Of prejudice and pride!

Weep for the child that day it learns
   Its father's feet have passed
Beyond the pale whence none return
   Save as a cowed outcast.

Weep not for me; for always, wife,
   The angry coals of shame
Burn deepest in the guileless life
   That bears the branded name.

54 *In the early 1900s, the Chester County Jail in Pennsylvania operated
under a modified version of the old Pennsylvania system of discipline
—separation of inmates by day and night with labor for the worthy.
Prisoners remained in their cells for all meals and even during the*

Sunday religious services which were delivered from the central hall. The principal work was handweaving: rag rugs on order and for general sale in Philadelphia, material for prison clothing and sheets. Women inmates sewed the uniforms by hand; there were no machines for use by the prisoners.

The dolls pictured on the following page were made by Mamie Slater for the daughter of the warden around 1905. Dressed as prisoners—the cloth was woven in the jail—they represent Mrs. Slater and her husband who was also confined. Mrs. Slater took hair for the woman doll from her own head; she also put a penny in the apron pocket.

55 *Over twenty thousand textile workers of Lawrence, Massachusetts, went out on strike in January 1912; wages had been lowered and the operation speeded up. The strike was painstakingly organized by the IWW to avoid lawlessness and violence and to provide food and fuel for the wageless families. After two months they achieved their goal, but not before dynamite had been planted by antistrikers to discredit the workers; workers' children had been prevented by club-wielding police and militia from finding refuge in outside communities; and the IWW leaders Joseph J. Ettor and Arturo Giovannitti had been arrested as accessories to murder. In a clash between police and strikers, a woman worker had been shot.*

While in jail awaiting the trial that would acquit both himself and Ettor, Giovannitti wrote several poems. In her introduction to the volume in which they were printed, Helen Keller commented:
"No one has ever given me a good reason why we should obey unjust laws. But the reason why we should resist them is obvious. . . . The dignity of human nature compels us to resist what we believe to be wrong and a stumbling-block to our fellow men."

One of the most famous of Giovannitti's poems is "The Walker." It says much about the play of incarcerated senses and the imagining spirit. The first two and the last of nine stanzas follow.

110

I hear footsteps over my head all night.

They come and they go. Again they come and they go all night.

They come one eternity in four paces and they go one eternity in four paces, and between the coming and the going there is Silence and the Night and the Infinite.

For infinite are the nine feet of a prison cell, and endless is the march of him who walks between the yellow brick wall and the red iron gate, thinking things that cannot be chained and cannot be locked, but that wander far away in the sunlit world, each in a wild pilgrimage after a destined goal.

Throughout the restless night I hear the footsteps over my head.

Who walks? I know not. It is the phantom of the jail, the sleepless brain, a man, the man, the Walker.

One-two-three-four: four paces and the wall.

One-two-three-four: four paces and the iron gate.

He has measured his space, he has measured it accurately, scrupulously, minutely, as the hangman measures the rope and the gravedigger the coffin—so many feet, so many inches, so many fractions of an inch for each of the four paces.

One-two-three-four. Each steps sounds heavy and hollow over my head, and the echo of each step sounds hollow within my head as I count them in suspense and in dread that once, perhaps, in the endless walk, there may be five steps instead of four between the yellow brick wall and the red iron gate.

My brother, do not walk any more. It is wrong to walk on a grave. It is a sacrilege to walk four steps from the headstone to the foot and four steps from the foot to the headstone.

If you stop walking, my brother, no longer will this be a grave, for you will give me back my mind that is chained to your feet and the right to think my own thoughts.

I implore you, my brother, for I am weary of the long vigil,
  weary of counting your steps, and heavy with sleep.
Stop, rest, sleep, my brother, for the dawn is well nigh and it is
  not the key alone that can throw open the gate.

56 *The Nebraska State Penitentiary, established 1869, "is located in a
suburb called Lancaster, or rather, Lancaster is located at the penitentiary, for outside of the prison there is but little else at Lancaster."
So wrote Walter Wilson in his satirical exposé of that institution in
1913; it is still an accurate description of many securely isolated
American prisons. During his investigation, Wilson found incised on
the walls these telling graffiti: the first is from a cell, the second from
a corridor.*

My prison cell was small and dingy
With here a bug and there a jigger,
The architect must been quite stingy
Or surely he would planned it bigger.
Soon roam I free beneath the stars,
And with pure joy my heart does swell,
Because I hate them prison bars,
That kept me in that awful little cell.

Here in this pen there is a place
Far worse than inquisition
Where judgment is a damning lie
That leads us to perdition.

A man is slowly tortured here
Within this hall of horror
As shrieks of anguish testify
As witness of his terror.

You scoundrels, rascals, villains, fiends
You demons proud and clever
Who drain a convict's life and blood,
May you go to hell forever.

57 *In order to execute his duties properly as chairman of the New York*
State Commission of Prison Reform in 1912, Thomas Mott Osborne
was voluntarily himself incarcerated in the Auburn Prison for one
week. His experiences led him to the conviction that prisoners must
be treated as human beings with practice in making responsible
decisions if they were to become, when restored to society, productive
law-abiding citizens. He devised the Mutual Welfare League, a form
of self-government and self-improvement, and with the warden's
help, instituted it first at Auburn and then as warden himself at Sing
Sing. Its motto was "Do Good; Make Good."

The following is part of an essay written in 1915 by Steven
Nemeth, 64338, Shoe [shop] 1, Cell 855, Sing Sing, in response to
a prize offered for the best account of the aims of the league. He had
learned English in the previous nineteen months, thanks to the
Osborne system.

When I came here I was crushed in spirit, broken in body and
full of bitterness against everybody, same as most of the men
who came here. The old system existed. The rules of this Prison
were very strictly and unhuman. In the shoe shop where I
worked were three keepers but the days could not passed
without fighting with knives or other instrument and sometime
the fight were very bloody. Smokking, newspaper reading talking
in shops mess-hall or in the marching line and moving, walking
in the shops was forbidden. We worked very little and we did
not work well and some time we wasted the raw material and

damaged the state property, because the rage and bitterness was so great in the man's heart against the prison officials and against the society who sent us here with long sentences, that we could not fight against our own feelings.

Every day at 4 clock we were locked up and we have only a few slices of bread and tea for supper. The cells were dampf and musty without air and so in the summer it was hot in the winter it was too cold and suffered much. Hollidays and Sundays were the worst. locked up 24- to 48 hours. When we came out the next morning every one of were nearly crazy, unsound in mind by the different kind of drugs that we used on them days. In these days the biggest trouble in the shops and all over the prison. The drug using made many of us crazy and many got different sickness from it. . . .

About a year ago came Mr. Osborne . . . and presented us with his confidence and founded our faithful friend the M.W.L. a new epoch is started with the league.

It is a body of prison self government. The shops are represented by delegates according to the number of inmates working in each shops. The league has its own constitution and governed by 9 members of the executive boards, elected among the delegates. They make the rules and consult in every thing with the warden. . . .

The new sustem of the League made a great change all over in the prison. We do not use drugs any more. Our excited temper became calme and so in the show shop in this year was not a single fight and only a very few happened in the other shops. Now every body willing to work and we do our work with care and willingly. Everybody is content with the situation, work with pleasure and this way we produced 50% more shoes than the other year. . . .

In the different kind of schools we mak up our defective study and every evening we have very interesting and sometime joyfully time, when we forget our past and we think only for better future. . . .

They would be some of us also would fail, and that is only shows how much we need the helpful hands of the people and the necessary means. The league could not exist without the aid of society. They must give work to us when we leave this place. . . .

58 *There was a depression in the United States in 1914 and workers lost their jobs, their homes, and their credit at the grocery store. There were many strikes. Joe Hill (born Joseph Hillstrom in Sweden), labor's most famous songwriter, participated in those against the copper mine owners of Utah. Shortly afterward he was arrested for the murder of a storekeeper and his son and was sentenced to death. Despite intervention by President Wilson, the Swedish government, and Australian as well as American workers, he was executed. Utah law allowed a condemned man to name his form of death; Joe Hill chose shooting as he believed himself to be a prisoner of class war. A stethoscope and a white paper heart were attached to his breast. Five marksmen pulled their triggers—four guns had dumdum bullets, one a blank—and in seventy seconds the attending doctor pronounced Joe Hill's body dead; as an American legend he lives on.*

During his two years in the Salt Lake County Jail Hill composed a number of songs; "It's a Long Way Down the Soup Line" to the tune of "Tipperary" was perhaps the most popular. He also continued his involvement in labor organization. The following letter gives advice to the editors of the IWW's Little Red Song Book.

Salt Lake County Jail
Nov. 29, 1914

Editor Solidarity:
    I see in the "Sol" that you are going to issue another edition of the Song Book, and I made a few changes and corrections

which I think should improve the book a little, which I am enclosing herewith.

Now, I am well aware of the fact that there are lots of prominent rebels who argued that satire and songs are out of place in a labor organization and I will admit that songs are not necessary for the cause; and whenever I "get the hunch" I intend to make some more foolish songs, although I realize that the class struggle is a very serious thing.

A pamphlet, no matter how good, is never read more than once, but a song is learned by heart and repeated over and over; and I maintain that if a person can put a few cold, common sense facts into a song, and dress them (the facts) up in a cloak of humor to take the dryness off of them, he will succeed in reaching a great number of workers who are too unintelligent or too indifferent to read a pamphlet or an editorial on economic science.

There is one thing that is necessary in order to hold the old members and to get the would-be members interested in the class struggle and that is entertainment. The rebels of Sweden have realized that fact, and they have their blowouts regularly every week. And on account of that they have succeeded in organizing the female workers more extensively than any other nation in the world. The female workers are sadly neglected in the United States, especially on the West coast, and consequently we have created a kind of one-legged, freakish animal of a union, and our dances and blowouts are kind of stale and unnatural on account of being too much of a "buck" affair; they are too lacking the life and inspiration which the woman alone can produce.

The idea is to establish a kind of social feeling of good fellowship between the male and female workers, that would give them a little foretaste of our future society and make them more interested in the class struggle and the overthrow of the old system of corruption. I think it would be a very good idea to use our female organizers, Gurley Flynn, for instance, *exclusively* for the building up of a strong organization among the female workers. They are more exploited than the men, and John Bull is willing to testify to the fact that they are not lacking in militant and revolutionary spirit.

By following the example of our Swedish fellow workers, and paying a little more attention to entertainment with original song and original stunts and pictures, we shall succeed in attracting and interesting more of the young blood, both male and female, in the One Big Union.

Yours for a change,
Joe Hill

59 *In 1874, when he was fourteen years old, Jesse Harding Pomeroy was sentenced to death as a vicious child mutilator and killer; the merciful authorities changed the sentence to life in solitary confinement. After forty years he was allowed to join the general prison population, but he was never set free; he died at the age of seventy-eight, having served fifty-eight years for crimes of which he maintained innocence.*

While in solitary he studied an exhaustive variety of subjects and wrote poems, stories, essays, and conundrums, many of which were printed under the name of Grandpa in The Mentor, *the inmate magazine of the Massachusetts State Prison at Charlestown. He kept contact, too, with outside political and domestic affairs; his first poem after release from solitary was entitled "A la Miss Suffragette." "My mind is my own making," he wrote, "and I am thankful for a good education—my own effort."*

Following are some mind-exercising mathematical puzzles.

Nightcaps for Nightgowns
March 25, 1916

When two numbers you shall write,
Four you stare at, and I am right;
If from that four, five you take,
One is left and no mistake.
     What are the numbers?
Ans. IV, = 4: take away V five, leaves one.

We have a word in our speech,
Which as writ, no thing can teach;
If now to it, one you prefix,
It then means, cross as two sticks.
     Name word, and meaning.
Ans. Word 0 zero: prefix 1 = 10 = X as two sticks.

There is a number that we use;
Now multiply it as you choose;
Add the answer,—'tis no trouble—
Finds that number or some double!
'Tis a magic number we here choose;
Please name it, 'tis in daily use.
The only one our language knows.
     What is it?
Ans. 9. Multiply by any number and add;
the result is always 9 or some multiple of 9:
$9 \times 2 = 18$: 1 and 8 = 9 etc.

60 *During the years 1913 to 1919 the women suffragists of America united in an intensive militant campaign for full political enfranchisement. They wrote, they lectured, they marched, and they picketed the Capitol and the White House. They kept vigil over*

watchfires and burned an effigy of President Wilson recalling the razing of George III's statue in 1776. Because they emphasized the absurdity of pursuing a war for democracy abroad when women were denied participation in their government at home, they were branded unpatriotic and even dangerously subversive. They were subjected to ridicule and to physical abuse and they were herded into jail. In prison, they protested unjust and unsanitary conditions, composed witty songs, and fasted. Released, they toured the country in a railroad car called the Prison Special, and wore their prison uniforms to dramatize the unjust imprisonment of suffragist demonstrators. It was not until 1920 that American women finally got the vote.

Rose Winslow was one of the movement's powerful forces. She had immigrated as a child from Poland and had worked fourteen hours a day in Pennsylvania hosiery mills from the time she was eleven years old until she contracted tuberculosis at nineteen. In 1917 she was arrested while picketing for voting rights and received a seven-month sentence for obstructing traffic. The following notes were smuggled out of the Washington, D.C., jail where she and other suffragists had undertaken a hunger strike for recognition as political prisoners.

If this thing is necessary we will naturally go through with it. Force is so stupid a weapon.

I know you won't get me out. That would be puny. I know you won't do it. My fainting probably means nothing except that I am not strong after these weeks. I know you won't be alarmed.

I was getting frantic because you seemed to think Alice was with me in the hospital. She was in the Psychopathic ward. The same doctor feeds us both, and told me. Don't let them tell you we take this well. Miss Paul vomits much. I do, too, except when I'm not nervous, as I have been every time but one. The feeding gives me a severe headache. My throat aches afterward, and I always weep and sob to my great disgust, quite against my will. I try to be less feeble minded. It's the nervous reaction, and I can't control it much. I don't imagine bathing one's food in tears is very good for one.

We think of the coming feeding all day. It is horrible. The doctor thinks I take it well. I hate the thought of Alice Paul and the others if I take it well.

We still get no mail; we are 'insubordinate.' It's strange, isn't it; if you ask for food fit to eat, as we did, you are 'insubordinate'; and if you refuse food you are 'insubordinate.' Amusing. I am really all right. If this continues very long I perhaps won't be. I am interested to see how long our so-called 'splendid American men' will stand for this form of discipline.

All news cheers one marvelously because it is hard to feel anything but a bit desolate and forgotten here in this place.

All the officers here know we are making this hunger strike that women fighting for liberty may be considered political prisoners; we have told them. God knows we don't want other women ever to have to do this over again.

61 *There was great national enthusiasm for the "war to end all wars"; those who opposed it overtly were socially and legally persecuted. The lot of the conscientious objector was particularly difficult. Ernest L. Meyer, a junior at the University of Wisconsin, rejected both combatant and noncombatant service on philosophical grounds. He was expelled from the university as dangerous and unpatriotic and was subsequently interned at Camp Taylor, Camp Sherman, Fort Leavenworth, and Fort Riley. Jeerers called "Yellowback! yellowback! We'll get you when we get back!" His sense of isolation was inten-*

sified because, although confined with religious objectors—Mennonites, Molokans, Christadelphians, Plymouth Brethren, Adventists, Quakers, members of the Church of God, the Church of Christ, the Apostolic Faith, and the House of David—he was neither one with them nor understood by them.

The following was written on August 27, 1918, the day the board appointed by the President of the United States, represented by Dean Harlan Stone of the Columbia Law School, held a hearing of the war objectors at Camp Sherman.

August 27.—This is written by the light of a candle in a tent musty with the smell of damp blankets, wet clothes and the acrid odor of mud. Across from me, seated on one cot, are my three Mennonite tent-mates, listening to one of them, Yoder, read from the Bible. The boys' faces are more than ordinarily grave, and there is a special heaviness in Yoder's voice as he reads the narrative of the Saviour's walk to Golgotha. The silence is invaded only by his voice and the rain plopping on the canvas and splashing in the pool under the ridge outside. The neighboring tents, too, are silent. When I thrust my head out of the door a moment ago I heard no hymns or hallelujahs anywhere; the whole Crusaders' colony is wet, desolate and quiet. Perhaps they all are praying as Yoder is praying, leaning on Heaven for help.

Well, they have need of it to-night. We passed today through the third degree; our consciences have been officially weighed and analyzed, and you shall soon learn, dear wife, whether to write me here or in the guardhouse. I confess I share the heaviness that presses upon my religious friends; though the thought of prison has almost become too familiar to be frightening. Perhaps it is only the eternal rain, and my loneliness. I can speak neither the tongue of the Crusaders nor the jargon of the military men.

62   *Eugene V. Debs, whose much quoted words, "While there is a lower
class I am in it; while there is a criminal element I am of it; while
there is a soul in prison I am not free," are as timely today as they
were when they were spoken, served his first jail term in 1894 as a
result of his participation in the workers' strike against the Pullman
Palace Car Company. In 1918 he was arrested under the Espionage
Act for a speech which allegedly obstructed military recruiting. He
was sentenced to ten years' imprisonment and was first sent to the
West Virginia Penitentiary at Moundsville and then to the Atlanta
Federal Penitentiary. From behind bars at Atlanta, Debs ran for
president of the United States on the Socialist ticket for the fifth time.
Debs was pardoned by President Harding at Christmas in 1921. He
sent his five dollars' release money to the Sacco and Vanzetti Defense Fund.*

*The following letter written from Atlanta to the Moundsville
warden illustrates well the extraordinary kindliness and generosity
that endeared Debs to so many Americans. Debs had been transferred from the state to a federal facility because the president of the
West Virginia State Board of Control had complained to the United
States Superintendent of Prisons that the extra guard force he believed necessary for Debs's and the other prisoners' safety cost the
prison five hundred dollars a month.*

Mr. J. Z. Terrell
Warden W. Va. Penitentiary
Moundsville W. Va.

Atlanta Ga. June 27th 1919

Mr. dear Mr. Terrell,

It has taken me some little time to get myself adjusted here
or you would have heard from me more promptly. The trip here
was without incident. Marshal Smith and his deputies treated
me very kindly and did all they could to make the trip pleasant
for me.

The check you were kind enough to send me was duly

received and has been placed to my credit. For this and the many other kindnesses I received at your hands I beg you to accept my warmest thanks. The personal effects you sent to my home reached there in good order, as I am advised by Mrs. Debs.

It was with real regret that I parted with you and that fine and manly son of yours on that to me eventful morning. How proud you and Mrs. Terrell must be of that beautiful boy!

My stay with you at the Moundsville prison will always be to me a source of satisfaction and inspiration. This may seem strange to those who are lacking in sympathy and understanding in such a situation, but it is nevertheless true. The Moundsville Prison under your enlightened and humane direction and ministration was to me a study of the deepest interest and I profited immeasurably by my experience there. From the moment of my arrival, when you personally received me, until I bade you good-bye, you treated me with uniform kindness and with all the consideration the rules would allow, as you did every other inmate of the prison, doing the very best you could to help and encourage them all, and for this I shall always hold you in grateful remembrance. . . .

I am getting along well here. The work is light and agreeable and the treatment all I could expect. With kindest regards and Warmest wishes, Yours faithfully,

Eugene V. Debs

63 *Kate Richards O'Hare was rich, handsome, well connected, and an international secretary of the Socialist party, for which she was also a popular and indefatigable lecturer. In 1917 she was arrested in the small town of Bowman, South Dakota, supposedly for an antiwar speech she had written, memorized, and delivered countless times*

throughout the country; it is generally accepted that her arrest was primarily a means of settling local political scores.

Nevertheless, she was sentenced to five years in the Jefferson City, Missouri, State Penitentiary. Women's work there was the stitching of "another-pair-if-sewing-rips" overalls. It was a heavy, grinding task; "the law of the shop," she wrote, "is the absolute limit of human endurance." Later she protested that she was taught criminality in that shop, for, against state law, the women were required to sew a wide variety of private company labels into the prison-made garments.

These are excerpts from letters to her "dear Sweethearts," her husband and their four children.

I am still fairly well, but beginning to feel the inevitable sense of weakness from the enervating effect of heat and lack of air. There are sixty women in the shop and seven half-windows, and they are placed at least ten feet above the floor and therefore useless as a means of ventilation. There are three very antiquated fans whose ancient and creaking joints sing an everlasting wailing song of protest, but they are all bunched over the matron's desk and the lower end of the room is absolutely without means of ventilation. The one full-sized window in the shop is right beside my machine and it is the only possible means of securing a direct current of air through the shop, but it is nailed down good and tight and the glass has been painted thickly over, making it utterly useless either for light or air. As a result we are forced to work all the time in the heat and glare of artificial light. Recently the foreman, who is not a bad sort of kid, chanced to be in a good humor and I asked him why the window had been made useless and suggested that the architect had evidently meant it to provide light and ventilation and asked him to have it opened. He consulted the shop matron and reported that it was impossible. When I insisted on a reason, he said that there was a legend that once upon a time a girl inmate had committed the heinous crime of smiling out of that window at a male inmate on the other side. Naturally, rampant virtue was outraged and from that day down to this, all women have been punished for that crime. . . .

We spend nine hours at the machine, and the other time locked in a crowded cell. On Monday and Tuesday we have one hour in the yard, on Wednesday less than half an hour, on Thursday and Friday no recreation whatever, Saturday we have three hours in the park and on Sunday from two to three hours in the courtyard. The little time we have in the yard is from five to six and that is the very hottest part of the day. It is absolutely impossible to walk in the broiling sun on the blistering cement pavement so we hug the hot wall as closely as possible for a bit of shade. No seats are provided and after our long day in the hot shop we go to the hotter courtyard and sit on the pavement or the tiny strip of ground bare of everything but broken brick, bits of rock and broken bottles. At the park we might really get a little real exercise but the space that we are permitted to cover is so circumscribed that it really amounts to the same old milling round and round like squirrels in a cage. I really think I have suffered more from lack of exercise than any other one thing; you know I was always passionately fond of walking, and the utter lack of opportunity to move about hurts me dreadfully.

Another painful condition has developed that troubles me somewhat. Our machines are old, decrepit and in the most deplorable condition of repair. They rattle and shake from the palsy of age and misuse and you can imagine what that does to the nerves of a person who knows as much of mechanics as I do and has due respect for good machinery and a passion for working with good tools. I have had my years of training in the machine shop and the youth who is our "boss" is as innocent of any knowledge of mechanics as he is of everything else. I am not permitted to make the slightest adjustment or even clean the machine, and I used it three months with never a cleaning. There is a knee-press by which we raise the pressure foot with our knee instead of our hand. In order to free the very heavy material under the feed and cross seams without knotting the thread or breaking the needle we must always keep our knee against this press. It beats a constant tattoo on our flesh and this has developed ugly and severely painful varicose veins where the press strikes my knee. So you see that I will carry the scars of this experience to my grave, not only mental and spiritual scars but physical ones as well.

The excessive heat of the early part of the week was deadly also and had its effect in pulling down my strength, but most of all I have suffered from lack of sleep. It was not only the ordeal of trying to sleep in the stifling cell where the steel walls were so hot you could not touch them, but the suffering of those about me was harder to bear. The poor Indian girl who is dying of syphilis is finding it so terribly hard to die. She has all the stamina of her race and the battle between the white man's disease and the Indian's firm hold on life is a sickening thing to witness! What strange problems we have in ethics, morals and humanity! Society shuts this poor girl up in prison because she killed the man who contaminated her; we force her to live thro long years of living hell, eaten by a loathsome disease and crushed by our prison system, a frightful menace to all who come near her, and our sense of humanity compels medical science to prolong the agony as long as possible. How different the ethics of the Indian, who ended the misery of hopelessly incurable and suffering.

Z. seemed glad that I was "philosophical." Yes, I am as philosophical as my physical discomforts will permit me to be, and after the grilling day in the shop I array myself in a shocking state of undress, sit in my little rocker and read with vast amusement and many chuckles the capitalist newspapers. It is joy pure and unalloyed to me to peruse the piteous squeaks and despairing wails of the erstwhile arrogant "press." The antics of the wise men in Washington remind me very much of the senseless scuttling about of the army of cockroaches that I uncover when I lift a book or paper in my cell. How shriekingly funny is all the wild hullabaloo about the "profiteers," and poor Rose Pastor Stokes got ten years for mildly suggesting that there were such animals in a most ladylike little note.

64 *Huddie Ledbetter, or "Leadbelly," was born to a respected farmer in 1885 in the Cado Lake district of Louisiana. During his early years he mastered the twelve-string guitar and was a partner of the blues singer Blind Lemon Jefferson. He roamed, drank, gambled, and loved, and in 1918 he was sentenced to thirty years in the Texas State Penitentiary at Huntsville for murder and assault to murder; the dead man had wanted his girl. After six weeks in prison Leadbelly escaped, using his great physical strength, but he was recaptured. He then devised a different technique for release; he dedicated a song to Governor Pat Neff, who was so delighted that he pardoned him. When Leadbelly was serving a second term in Louisiana, he redid the song for Governor O. K. Allen, recording it for John A. Lomax who took it to him; he was again released. The original version as sung to John A. Lomax follows.*

Nineteen Hundred and Twenty-Three,
The judge took my liberty away from me.
Left my wife wringin' her hands an' cryin',
"Lawd have mercy on de man of mine."
Spoken: Bud Russell had me goin' on down. I couldn' do
            nothin' but look back at her. He had chains all around

my neck an' couldn' do nothin' but wave my hands. I
look back at her an' here what I tole her.
Tole my wife 'fore I lef' the lan',
Never no more see her, do the bes' she can.
Spoken: Her name was Mary, I look back at Mary.
Goodby, Mary,
Oh, Mary.
I am your servant compose this song,
Please Governor Neff lemme go back home. (Had thirty-five
years.)
I am your servant compose this song,
Please Governor Neff let me go back home.
I know my wife will jump and shout,
Train rolls up I come steppin' out.
Spoken: I know she be pretty glad. I know I be glad, myself.
I know my wife'll jump and shout,
When the train rolls up and I come steppin' out.
Spoken: I look around and begin to thank Governor Pat Neff. I
wanted him to have a little mercy on me because I had
thirty-five years.
Please Honorable Governor be good and kind,
Have mercy on my great long time.
Please Governor Neff be good and kind,
Have mercy on my great long time.
Spoken: They turn loose some on pardon, some on parole. Some
they's cuttin' they time.
I don' see to save my soul,
Don' git a pardon, try me on a parole.
Spoken: He ask me where did you want to go an' here what I
tole him.
Goin' back to Mary,
Oh, Mary,
Lawdy, Mary,
Um, um, um.

Some folks say it's a sin,
Got too many wimmen an' too many men (In the pen).
Some folks say it's a sin,
Got too many wimmen an' too many men.
Spoken: I want to talk to him 'bout my time again. If he didn'
cut it he might pardon it.
Please Honorable Governor be good an' kind,
If don' get a pardon, will you cut my time? (Give me a pardon.)
Please Honorable Governor be good an' kind,
If don' get a pardon, will you cut my time?
Spoken: Here's the las' words I said to him.
Had you Governor Neff like you got me,
Wake up in the mornin' an' I'd set you free.

65   *Charles Chapin, Sing Sing 69690, was a privileged prisoner. Formerly city editor of the* New York World, *he had killed his wife to
whom he had been married for thirty-nine years to protect her from
want and disgrace when he lost most of his fortune speculating in
sugar stocks. Finding him depressed by life inside, Warden Lewis E.
Lawes put him in charge of the* Bulletin, *the prison newspaper, and
when that was forced to close, allowed him with the help of outside
contributors and convict labor to transform the barren prison yard
into an enormous garden. In a triumphant letter to the editor of*
House and Garden, *Chapin described the hundreds of rose bushes,
thousands of bulbs, iris, peonies, and wide variety of exotic trees he
had planted, concluding with this* pièce de résistance: *"Can you
imagine how happy I am over the fact that our Warden is having a
greenhouse built for my exclusive use in a secluded spot where no
convict foot is permitted to intrude. I expect to spend most of my
working hours in it during the winter." Daily he brought fresh flowers
to Lawes's office and private house.*

But Chapin's energies were not to be confined by a hothouse and once more he organized willing and unwilling fellow convicts and charitable free world support to build this aviary as an embellishment to his garden; it took three years' hard labor.

66 Bartolomeo Vanzetti emigrated to America from northern Italy and worked at such jobs as pick and shovel man, pastry cook, and fish peddler. In 1920 he was arrested with Nicola Sacco for the murder of a pay master and his guard in South Braintree, Massachusetts. In spite of seriously conflicting evidence, they were found guilty. After his conviction he was confined in the Massachusetts State Prison at Charlestown where he worked in the license plate shop and the tailor shop. He was an avid reader and writer.

When he had been in prison for four years, Vanzetti developed what was thought to be stomach ulcers. He was sent first to the prison hospital, then to the Bridgewater State Hospital for the Criminal Insane. The following angry letter was written from that institution.

Dear Friend:

. . . Even before I came here, I was the cause of much disturbed fear; distrust of keepers and doctors who have their jobs, love them, and believe me and my friends the worst and dangerous criminals. The higher of them, the more jack-asses.

So it follows that I was kept in solitary confinement for five weeks, after which I was allowed to the day-room, where it is forbidden to speak, and watched by eyes always. A few days after that I was admitted to the common table; knives and forks were taken off from circulation, and we compelled to use the fingers as table-tools. Meanwhile, every good day, the other patients were compelled to go into the yard, and I had to stay in. It is five years that I have been deprived of all that makes life worth living. Sunlight and open-air is what is greatly needed after five years of shadows and miasmatic dwelling. So I kicked and I kicked: I want my rights, and I have the right to a daily hour in the open air. The State so splendidly framed us, cannot it give me any rights? Meanwhile, I began to perceive abuse and wrongs to the patients and, therefore, to protest and rebel. Were I alone, they would, for this, have me die within this wall. Well, after my protests, I was allowed to go into the yard; once a day, early in the morning, when none were there, and together with the biggest attendance. Thus, in three months, I went 7 times into the yard, and only the 7th I stayed there one hour, all the other, less. I used to clean the floors, help the patients take off the dust, watering plants, etc., so that the head assistant proclaimed me to the doctors "his better patient." And yet they kept watching, fearing and distrusting me to the point that the head assistant said that I should write in English my letters to my sister, to which I answered in rhymes. . . .

67 *Raised on his father's farms in the south of Italy, Nicola Sacco emigrated to Boston as a young man, found work in the area's shoe industry, and became an ardent anarchist. For the six years during which Sacco and Vanzetti's defense sought and was repeatedly denied a new trial, Sacco was incarcerated in the Dedham jail; he was not allowed to work as, due to a technicality, he was not yet sentenced. An affectionate man who loved all living and growing things, he suffered intensely from confinement. Separation from his beloved wife Rosa, his small son, and his daughter who was born four months after his arrest, was hard to bear.*

The following letter was written to Mrs. Cerise Jack, a member of the New England Civil Liberties Committee, who gave Sacco English lessons during the winter of 1924–1925.

November 12, 1926. Dedham Jail

Dear Friend Mrs. Jack:

I have not forgot you and not your dear household no, I haven't, and I want you to know that on the contrary often I were thinking of you, even in the sad days your image appear to my vision always with more vividly remembrance. . . . I could see your dear household, the green grass, the beautiful flowers and the lovely fruit trees that only Mr. Jack can take care.

For also, you will excuse my poor Shakespear English: poor, yes, because I have not get yet all the song and the harmony of this beautiful language, as I have promise you that some day I would have surprise you with one of my good English letter. But, I want you to believe me sincerely, my dear teacher, that if it didnt succeed at my promise it is not my fault. No, it isn't, because I have tryed with all my passion for the success of this beautiful language, not only for the sake of my family and for the promise I have made to you—but for my own individual satisfaction, to know and to be able to read and write correct English. But woe is me! It wasn't so; no, because the sadness of these close and cold walls, the idea to be away from my dear family, for all the beauty and joy of liberty—had more than once exhause my passion.

And then, you be surprise that after all these cruel and long sagragation years, they still have courage to bring me an English teacher—while they keeping my family away from me that I long so much to see them at least once a week. It is a real shame. Poor humanity! . . .

68 *A contributor to* Smart Set, Harper's Weekly, *and* The Nation, *publisher of the* Two Worlds *and* The Lyric, *and* Beau, *the man's magazine, Samuel Roth was apprehended in 1928 for the possession of obscene literature which agents of the New York Society for the Suppression of Vice apparently found in the dustbin of his wife's book shop; he also used the U.S. Postal Service to distribute such forbidden titles as* The Perfumed Garden. *Consequently he tenanted the Tombs, the Welfare Island prison, the U.S. Detention Headquarters on West Street in New York City, and a prison in Philadelphia. Caustically summing up his experiences, he wrote: "at least if a bed bug bites it does not do so with a mouth used in invoking holy prayers."*

The following excerpt is from Stone Walls Do Not. . . . The Chronicle of a Captivity, *which he had once thought "to spread throughout the land as a protest against shabby prison conditions," but which, disillusioned, he consented to have published in an edition of only one hundred and three copies.*

The Song of the River

Why, I wonder, do they always build jails either in a midst of sea, like the famous French prison on Devil's Island, or on the shores of a river, like Sing Sing or this jail of mine?

From where I sit on my cot I see the East River as she glides by, spangled with the multitudinous lights of Manhattan. Last night winds like furies lashed her into an abyss of such unutterable blackness that I could barely see across her.

Are jails built adjacent to waters so as to help to prevent the escape of their inmates? Then let me propound a purely moral question: why, if it is wrong for a prisoner to wish to escape from prison, is the temptation to escape made so strong and alluring? For nothing makes a man want to wander away far from where he happens to be, as much as a river, especially a river as restless, as carefree, as insistently rebellious with conflicting tides as this East River of ours!

I feel that I am at war with this river, for she mocks every reconciliation I try to make with this rotten cell of mine. Six in the mornings, when the prison bell breaks my sleep, I see her crawling along drowsily under the sceptical eye of the morning star, for it is not unknown to that wise planet that, flowing as she does from sea to sea, the East River accomplishes no significant journey such as is the pride of those self-made rivers that rise as mere springs in mountains many miles of journeying from the all-consuming sea. As I march along her bank at midday to perform some humble task assigned to me by the lords of my captivity, she is rolling along lazily at my side, murmuring casually such names as Bowling Green, Forty-Second Street, the Battery, and places it is not becoming a moral writer and a father of children to admit knowing. But it is at such times as this—when I have returned from the hateful tyranny to be locked up with myself for twelve of the most subtle and dangerous hours of the accursed day—that the brazenness of the river is most outspoken. . . .

69 *Robert Joyce Tasker committed and was convicted of armed robbery in 1924, just before his twenty-first birthday. He attributed his unusually heavy sentence, five years to life, to a nationwide reaction against youthful offenders caused by the Leopold and Loeb case. While at San Quentin he developed his writing skills and in 1927 sold an essay, "My First Day in Prison," to the* American Mercury. *It was the policy in the twenties of its editor, H. L. Mencken, to seek out works of unknown authors describing hitherto unheralded aspects of human life.*

Tasker's personal correspondence with Mencken illustrates many of the problems of prison authorship: that of materials—Tasker apologizes for pencil, he was "many hours away from ink"; his payments had to be sent directly to his father; he was unable to get a notary to witness a contract; he was afraid that too much publicity or aid from the literary world would jeopardize his hearing before the parole board: it was comprised of the same men who, because of general rioting in 1928, placed a ban on inmate writing.

The following autobiographical-psychological essay is an editorial that appeared in San Quentin's inmate publication The Bulletin; *under Tasker's leadership it achieved an unusually high level of professionalism.*

To just what degree a man in prison enjoys a change of character and intellect is not always an easy matter to determine. Almost invariably the prisoner becomes more tractable, diplomatic, and shrewd. But just what percentage of this is surface polish, and what mental revision, it is more difficult to learn. Even so, very few men are able to testify as to the change in themselves; the mind has a trick of remembering things in a complimentary light, completely forgetting more humiliating phases of the earlier creed.

In the interests of psychology, I have rooted back into the archives of this journal, picking out sundry articles, yarns, and verses, written by myself. They comment upon themselves.

Extending through all issues, from September of 1926 until the present writing, I find that I have written—an article upon crime causes, laying the blame at the door of the adventurous spirit in youth; a story, submitted in contest, in the best smart-alecky *Saturday Evening Post* manner, with no relation to crime or prison; a story, submitted in contest, in the best side-splitting western-story tradition; a phantasy about two youthful long-timers who are day-dreaming of liberty; a sort of kickback article in defense of the aforementioned phantasy, still insisting that prisoners *do* dream—that they are not altogether crass brutes; a story of a man who got shot in a revolution, which, although it didn't come off, was planned to ennoble revolutionists; a story about a careless father whose ways enabled his son to get into the hoosegow, much to the despair of law-and-order papa; a poem about an adventurous youth who came down from the hills and fell afoul of the gendarmes; a poem in radical format about the lithesome soul of a prisoner.

Comes next an article gibing at stupid reformers for having bored us to the extent of forcing us to read good literature to divert our ears from the apostolic din; an exceptionally lousy story about a man in love; . . . a sketch in metrical verse, and prose, in praise of a Bull Durham cigarette; a satire about a bad convict who escaped, but soon came yowling back to prison for protection against the modernists; an article pointing out that what is romantic to read about is not very pleasant to live; a protest against hysterical increase of the duration of prison sentences; a charge that "frat men" of colleges are as brutal as, and many times more so than convicts; a story about a boy who ran away from prison, and committed suicide rather than return; a philosophic consideration of prison life; an article concerning the sapping effects of a long term in prison; an article pointing out that a lock on the door of a palace makes a prison; an interview with a Prison Commissioner of Holland—his elegant beard still inspires me with awe; . . . notes as to the naivete of a long-timer upon being released from prison; a shy hint that needless energy is expended in vilifying prisoners which might well be directed toward allaying new crimes; notes on the dreams and aspirations of prisoners; weary speculations as to the culmination of the crime problem.

All these have character significance, but just what significance I seem unable to decide. They are not all that I have written, for there have been scores of sports articles, amusement program reports, comments upon local events, book reviews. These recorded, are the things which will enable the psychologists to screw on their monocles, exclaiming, "Ah—and here we have the mental graph of a convict."

IV

The 86th Annual Report of the Prison Association of New York opens with an optimistic appraisal of its hope for "prison betterment" which might have been written today.

"The outbreaks in our prisons during the year 1929 aroused an unprecedented public interest and concern relative to the administrative features and the physical conditions in these institutions. This interest increased rapidly, and at the beginning of 1930 there was a strong public demand that something be done about our prisons. The press of the State rendered an unusual service in stimulating public interest in support of prison reform. This, coming also from the part of the press theretofore opposed to prison reform, was extremely encouraging. However, most promising of all was the attitude of the 1930 Legislature. From the beginning of the session it was evident to close observers that not only the Governor of the State but the Legislature was determined that the year should not pass without a decided forward step being made in the interest of better prisons and prison administration. Individuals, state departments, and organizations long advocating prison reform realized that the time had arrived for a substantial fulfillment of their recommendations, earnestly and patiently made over a period of years."

70 *Victor Nelson was handsome, persuasive, and intelligent, but he liked high life and liquor and found it easier to obtain them by stealing than by holding down a job. His long criminal career started when he was an adolescent; he was a prototype recidivist; for instance, almost immediately after he was paroled in the custody of reformer Thomas Mott Osborne, for whom he was to work as a librarian, he was convicted of assault and robbery.*

In 1931 Nelson wrote Prison Days and Nights *with the encouragement and guidance of the psychiatrist at the Norfolk County jail in Dedham, Massachusetts, who hoped he would find out from it how the prisoner really thinks. On the basis of the book, Nelson was paroled in charge of the doctor. The following is from its opening chapter.*

One o'clock. Back to work again. The same stuffy shops, the same tiresome work. It is absolute industrial masturbation! Merely working men in order to keep them busy, with no pride in the finished product, no care about inculcating habits of craftsmanship, no thought except to make us do something we don't like to do. The guards on their elevated benches become lazy-minded, unpremeditated sadists, and take a senseless delight in giving each man the job he most heartily hates to do. This comes from natural stupidity, prejudices racial and religious, and the fierce desire of the average man to savor power—when he gets a chance to use it. Lo, the poor guard! In his mind's eye he can see us as we were in the free world; with money, ravishing women, all the sensual delights which must be forever unattainable to him. We have had this. He has never had it, never will have it. Therefore, enviously, gloatingly, he exacts vengeance upon us for the unalterable deficiencies in his own life. . . .

Four o'clock. Yard time. Recreation. We go from the stuffy shop to the colorless yard. In it is no blade of grass, no tree, no bit of freshness or brilliance. Gray walls, dusty gravel, dirt and asphalt hardness. We walk about, or during our first few months or years manage to throw a ball back and forth and in some degree exercise our bodies. The longer we stay here, the less we do. At last we merely walk at a funeral pace, or lean against a wall and talk.

We always talk. During the working hours, but even more so during the cell hours, we store up facts, reflections, broodings, so that our minds are overflowing. And every chance we get to unburden them, we avail ourselves of it. We talk *at* each other. We do not converse; we deliver monologues in which we get rid of the stored-up bubblings. We try to live through words and self-dramatization. Our essential need is for actual tangible living, which we cannot have; so we try to live by pretending to live in tall stories based on how we'd like to live, how we long to live.

Four-thirty. Yard time is over. We march to our cells, taking with us the evening meal. The shop has been so enervating, so weakening, so downright devitalizing, that we are glad to go to our cells. We think, "Well, here's another day done. Another day nearer home. God, but it's good to get back to the cell!" In our hearts, however, we know that the cell is even worse than the shop; and that in the morning we'll be saying, "God, but it's good to get out of that damned cell!"

71   *This song was sung by an inmate called King Kong on the Pontiac, Illinois, prison farm.*

How will it end?
Ain't got a friend.
My only sin is in my skin
What did I do, babe,
To be so black and blue.

72 *The writer of the following letter was a protégé of Margaret Sanger,*
who had served thirty days in 1917 for opening an illegal birth control
clinic in Brooklyn. She undoubtedly empathized with the plight of
prisoners, for she wrote several letters that were instrumental in
obtaining the release of this inmate.

Box B
Dannemora, N.Y.
December 27, 1940

Dear Mrs. Sanger:

Received your lovely box of chocolates and can't find words
to express my feelings. Tears of happiness came to my eyes for
the second time in one day, but I am getting ahead of my story.

First of all Christmas morning we had a High Mass, about
1,400 men attended. I sing in the fine choir we have and after
mass the chapalin called me to one side and let me read a
wonderful letter he recieved from Mr. Macdonald in it he told
father Hyland how I was to be given a labor job at .40¢ per
hour and would be given the same chance for advancement as
any other man on the job. No one will know about my past
record. He then went on and told what a fine woman you were
and he said he didn't believe I would ever fail you.

After a fine dinner we saw a good movie, then came back to
our cells. It seemed everyone was getting letters or boxes of
candy from home—that is everyone but me. Then my number
was called and I recieved your gift tears came to my eyes, I had
no more than dried them and I was called again I recieved
another gift and letter from the Priest back home who was with
my dear Mother when she died a year ago last April. I had to
dry my eyes again. It was so sweet of you to remember me and
bring me such cheer and happyness.

Doctor Joseph Moore, chairman of the Parole Board told me
that he knew you and wondered why you were helping me, I

explained every thing to him and he told me he did not think Mr. Macdonald really wanted to give me a job, but was only making the offer to please you. I tried to tell him that was not true and showed him the letters Mr. Macdonald wrote to me. So he said he would look into the matter futher. I told this to the chapalin and he is doing everything within his power to help me. I believe Doctor Moore did not believe I told you the truth about myself and that I was arrested before. I hope he finds out in the near future that I did not lie to you, or to him and that I mean to live a good clean life when released. . . .

73 *In March 1942, Lieutenant General John L. DeWitt, commander of the Western Defense Command, ordered that all persons of Japanese descent, citizens as well as foreign-born, should be removed from strategic areas along the West Coast. By August over 100,000 Japanese had been concentrated in assembly centers or in relocation camps. The former were temporary locations, mostly race tracks and fairgrounds in which many internees lived in stables and livestock shelters; the latter were hastily erected barracks cities. This invasion of constitutional rights was justified on grounds of military expediency.*

The Japanese with great resilience and ingenuity and often with humor adjusted as best they could to incarceration. They organized self-government systems, schools, and entertainments; they gardened both for food and for beauty; and they published newspapers and magazines.

One of the assembly centers was at the Santa Anita Race Track. Its first occupants were brought from the Los Angeles harbor area on April 3, 1942; its population rose swiftly to 18,770. By April 18 it had a newspaper, the Santa Anita Pacemaker; *it was issued twice weekly and given to each household as a public service until October 7, when virtually all the Santa Anitans had been distributed to one of the ten relocation centers in eastern California, Idaho, Utah, Arizona, Wyoming, Colorado, and Arkansas.*

These articles are from the July 25, 1942, edition of the Pacemaker.

DRAINAGE CURE SOUGHT. Shower, Washday Regulations set.

To ease the cesspool drainage problem, a schedule of closed days for laundries and showers was announced today by H. Russell Amory, Center Manager.

All laundries will be closed each Wednesday while showers will shut down in accordance with the following schedule:

Shower No. 1, 5 Porter's Cap—Saturday
Shower No. 2 Southend of Seabiscuit—Sunday
Shower No. 3 Seabiscuit and He Did—Friday
Shower No 4 32 Whirlaway—Thursday
Shower No. 5 37 Equipoise—Monday
Shower No. 6 15 Third Street—Tuesday
Main Shower Front of Grandstand—Wednesday

NISEI COUPLE WED IN MISSOURI

Springfield, Mo., July 25. Private Alan N. Teranishi, 26, stationed at O'Reilly hospital here, and Lillian M. Kodama, 24, of Reedley, Calif., were married at the County Courthouse here this week with the blessings of the FBI and the County Attorney's office.

The couple, both Nisei, were married by County Judge Frank Wheeler.

Her marriage saved Miss Kodama from having to go to an assembly center with her parents, the bridegroom told county officials.

RUGS BY-PRODUCT OF CAMOUFLAGE

Latest by-products of the camouflage net project are the

colorful rugs made from tie strings of the gauze masks discarded by workers.

One of the clever rug makers is Yasuko Yuasa of 7–4–7, who has knitted a rug two and a half feet long and two feet wide. She plans to make it longer as soon as she collects more tie strings.

Yasuko, who works on crew 49, has all her fellow workers saving masks for her. She says the brighter the colors, the more tie strings are valued by the girls.—by Emi Kusumi.

EDITORIAL
Second Front Now for Victory

A recent letter to President Roosevelt from 45 residents of the Tanforan assembly center reads, "Because of our situation, we regret we have not been able as yet to participate in the war effort of this country in the way of production and combat. . . . It is our conviction that this people's war must end in victory for the Allied Nations. . . . We therefore call for an offensive— A SECOND FRONT NOW—for Victory."

That the evacuees are in accord with the views voiced by American leaders is an indication that, in spite of being denied active participation in the total war against fascism, they are not unaware of the war and all that America's victory means.

Their letter is in agreement with the views of Vice President Henry Wallace who says: "The time to strike hard is rapidly approaching. By doing so, I am convinced that our total eventual losses will be reduced and victory hastened."

It is America's victory we want—without delay.

74 *The contribution of prisoners throughout the United States to win-ning World War II was great. They bought war bonds, gave blood, and with their savings financed a bomber that was named after an*

inmate who had died in a medical research program. They also worked long overtime hours in the prison industries to get needed supplies to the armed forces. Draft boards came into the prisons and many men were released on enlisting. This page is from the May-June 1944 issue of The Atlantian, *the magazine of the Atlanta Federal Penitentiary.*

United States of America

MAY 31, 1944*

IN ACCOUNT WITH:

The Prisoners of the Atlanta Penitentiary

After THREE YEARS of War Effort.

Total production of war goods, in dollars (since April 1, 1941) This includes not only canvas cloth, but manufactured goods—tarpaulins, water tanks, mattresses and many other products.	$21,468,966.34
Total production of canvas, in yards	36,864,272
Total number of Bonds purchased	$102,750.00
Total amount of blood donated to the Red Cross plasma bank	1,571 pts.
Total amount of dollars donated to the Red Cross and other patriotic causes	$5,228.37
Total number of men "graduated" to actual war jobs in the outside world (Many others were released to work immediately contributant to the war job.)	1,093
Total number of men "graduated" into the armed services	141

. . . and SERVICES ARE CONTINUING.

NO STRIKES
NO ABSENTEEISM
NO SABOTAGE OR BOTCHED
WORK

* Exactly three years ago this month, seven months before Pearl Harbor, Atlanta's administration and men committed themselves to a program of all-out war effort. The above accounting is proof that Atlanta has never faltered or slackened in the fulfillment of its promise and responsibility.

75   *When in the late forties it became evident that the United States and Russia would not cooperate in peace as they had in war and that the Chinese Communists were driving the Nationalists from the mainland, the United States feared that Communists had also infiltrated the government and it commenced intensive investigations of its past and present employees. The atmosphere in which charges were made and prosecuted was highly emotional.*

In 1948 Whittaker Chambers told the House Committee on Un-American Activities that Alger Hiss, a former distinguished government servant and at the time president of the Carnegie Endowment for International Peace, had been a member of the Communist party. Later, after Hiss had sued him for libel, Chambers asserted that he and Hiss had engaged in espionage. Chambers, an avowed ex-Communist, swore at different times both that he had and had not collected dues from Hiss, that he had accepted Hiss's old car for party use, and had known him well socially. Hiss denied that he had ever been a member of the Communist party or engaged in espionage; he admitted to having known Chambers only slightly. Hiss stood two trials in 1949, much of the testimony revolving around the authorship of documents typed on a Woodstock typewriter similar or identical to one owned by Mrs. Hiss. Chambers alleged that he had secreted some of these papers and others that were photographed on microfilm in an abandoned dumbwaiter shaft. The microfilm was later hidden in a hollowed-out pumpkin.

Hiss was ultimately convicted of perjury and sentenced to five years imprisonment at the Lewisburg (Pa.) Federal Penitentiary. In prison he was not allowed to teach or work in the library, but was assigned to a manual labor job in the warehouse. He, like other prisoners, could correspond only with his family and his lawyers. The following letters were written jointly to his wife and their young son.

May 15, 1952—Thursday night

Dearest darlings,

Tony, my boy, that business on Park Ave. last Mon. must

have been quite a shock. Actually, like most cases of aggression or hostility it will cease to bother you as soon as you understand what made those two boys pick on you. Once you understand why someone does something strange or unfriendly it ceases to be strange; and it even ceases to be unfriendly when you see it isn't really directed at you because you're you at all. It is caused by something sick in the other fellow or by his being mixed up about something. Actually, I have met in here a great many fellows who have done things just like what was done to you and almost all of them have, nevertheless, some very, very good qualities. If those 2 boys had known you, I'm sure they would have liked you so much that they would have wanted to be your friends and then they wouldn't have dreamed of doing anything against you. One thing I'm sure of—they certainly needed the money even more than you did, poor as we are! Another thing I'm equally sure of—there must be people, grown ups, who have been much, much, meaner to them than they were to you. That's how they got that way, there's no doubt of it. So, seriously, I'm much sorrier for them than I am for you, though of course what I really mean is that I'm sorry people are so treated that they act that way. On the next visit you and I can compare our ideas of what they are really like and who or what taught them to be bullies, which is a very unhappy thing to be. . . .

June 22, 1952—Sunday
. . . Yesterday morning I saw a charming and amusing thing. A mother song sparrow was energetically seeking food. She popped in and out of a border of iris leaves, quickly (almost nervously) picking here and there in the ground. Now and again she would suddenly hop about this way and that on the nearby lawn—always intent solely on food. She was a pale tan-brown, trim, abrupt, precise. The whole time she was followed by a roly poly, slow, unsure baby who had the silliest stump of a new tail.

149

I was watching a lesson in getting lunch. The much darker, muddy colored little fatty was *NOT* a very good pupil (probably too well fed by mama to be hungry). He watched mama pretty closely—most of the time. And now and then he would take a slow and lazy peck at the ground. Every now and then his attention would wander and when he came to, mama would have moved off a couple of feet. Then he would run-waddle (he hadn't learned mama's abrupt, quick hop) after her as fast as he could until he was only about a foot away. Two or 3 times mama darted into the iris stalks while he was daydreaming and was no where to be seen when he woke up. Then he was panicky until he caught sight of her again and would pay much closer attention—*for a few minutes*. Once she bounced out of the iris with tubby left behind—probably woolgathering again. Suddenly he came scooting out as if he were being chased by a bull elephant, but as soon as he caught sight of active efficiently busy mama he slowed his hurrying pace and once more began his dawdling imitation of his mother, with frequent lapses of attention and occasional anxious scurryings to catch up again with her.

x-x-x It is now a little after 4. We spent the afternoon in the yard and watched a fairly good baseball game. I neglected to mention that yesterday morning the coolness kept most men indoors. As a result the bocci courts were empty and I played several games, first against the cabinet maker and then, when 2 others drifted over, with him as my partner in doubles. He plays his national game with serious intentness and uses his excellent judgment of distance and angle to good effect. Fortunately I did not let him down too badly (past experience in billiards helps me to judge the angles in the frequent "bank" shots that are called for) and we won handily against our novice opponents. . . . My 3 rose bushes still flourish and the lilies are dense. So much love, Alger—Daddy

76 *Thomas "Yonnie" Licavoli was a prohibition bootleg king; he estab-*
lished his empire by speedboating beer and whiskey from Canada to
Detroit and Toledo. In 1934 he was convicted of masterminding the
gangland murder of four, although at the time of the killing he was
at a funeral in another state.

Under Ohio law the parole board could examine a prisoner serving
a life sentence for first-degree murder after twenty years and, if it felt
he deserved a second chance, recommend that the governor reduce
the sentence to second-degree murder; he would then be eligible for
parole. Licavoli applied but was turned down; he was released on
lifetime parole in January 1972, after serving thirty-seven years.

The following is taken from Licavoli's carefully thought out state-
ment to the parole board in 1955, entitled "Resistance to Prison's
Defeat."

I am not ambitious as a writer. But in prison, as the reader will
realize, there exists slight opportunity for a man to get up and
speak his mind. It is one of prison's convictions that the man
who keeps his mouth shut is most certain to escape trouble. So,
most men learn quickly to remain inaudible. At my typewriter,
however, there was every opportunity for me to indulge in gay
and unrestrained explosions of emotions. My typewriter served
as a safety valve. The fact that I kept my waste-basket full of
the stuff I had written and discarded meant nothing, since I
had accomplished my purpose—which was to get the poison of
prison's restraint out of my system. I wrote about everything
conceivable. If I read something with which I disagreed, I sat
down and voiced my complaint in strong and sometimes violent
words—and then threw away what I had written, feeling much
better for having got the stuff out of my mind and body. It was
much like going out on the recreation field to play or watch a
game. Out there one could yell to the top of his lung power,
but the occasions came too infrequently. So, I used my

typewriter to do a bit of noiseless screaming! It worked—and it still does.

It gave me a system of ducking prison's punches that has served me well.

Stamp-collecting became another exciting diversion from prison. When I wasn't doing prison work, I collected and classified stamps. I wound up with a fine collection. Then I took to song-writing, again simply as an escape. I was successful in having a number published. And with both stamps and songs I learned much because I had to do a lot of studying. That was the real purpose—something for the mind, a fresh diet, far removed from prison.

I've followed sports of every kind, in newspapers, magazines, books and radio. Baseball, football, tennis, golf, even polo. I've kept records and my files have on occasions looked like the morgues of newspapers. Annually I've taken inventory of the files and filled waste-baskets with discarded stuff.

It has added up to a profitable business—that of winning a 20-year battle with prison.

I am still in prison, yes—physically, at least.

But in many ways I have lived outside of prison all these years. I had to live outside to EARN the right for consideration by society now.

It's my honest belief that I have earned that right.

Licavoli's enthusiasm and expertise in stamp collecting—in 1971 while still in prison he won the Joe Fitzpatrick Award at the New York Interpex for his display of space covers—spread to other inmates, and in 1958 they organized the Ohio Penitentiary Stamp Club. Ten years later the club had its own journal and in 1970 it held an exhibition—the second of its kind in the country—drawing exhibitors and visitors from both inside and outside the prison. This first-day cover marks the 1971 exhibit; it was designed by an inmate and bears the insignia of the club.

2-OPEX-71

OHIO'S Second Penal Exhibit

1971

77 *Caryl Chessman was found guilty on seventeen counts of kidnaping,*
robbery, grand theft, and sex offenses and sentenced to death by a
Los Angeles court in 1948. Although he admitted to a violent past,
he maintained that he was innocent of the crimes for which he was
convicted; he insisted he was not the "red-light bandit." Imprisoned
on San Quentin's death row, he devoted himself to his appeals and
to obtaining stays of execution. For most of the time he was his own
attorney. In order to win popular support for his case, he wrote the
best seller, Cell 2455, Death Row. *Authorities allowed him to write*
a second book but impounded both copies of the manuscript. It was
smuggled out on the carbon paper; every day the inmate trash detail
removed from his cell the basket of crumpled carbons, and soon after
they reached the publisher. In this book, Trial by Ordeal, *Chessman*
describes the therapeutic value of authorship. "Writing changed the

153

world for me. It proved a catharsis and more. It offered a chance to channel my drives and aggressions, to use them rather than be used by them." Chessman's execution date was set for the ninth time on the second of May 1960. Stay was denied and he was put to death in San Quentin's green-walled gas chamber. The following is from the final pages of Trial by Ordeal.

The dream had held me, fiercely, as an eagle holds its prey, and then it had slammed me awake, with the sickening force of a blow in the solar plexus.

The dream remained in the cell with me. The gas chamber was in the cell, too, and all the years I had spent on Death Row had been compressed into that frozen instant.

In the dream I had died, been put to death in a festooned execution cell, with the witnesses laughing and pointing. What followed was kaleidoscopic. The charivari, celebrating my death, was wild and frenzied. Speeches were cheered. Headlines screamed. Copies of my book were thrown into a blazing bonfire. Three little men, grotesquely costumed, weirdly masked, leaped up and down, crying, "We showed him! We showed him!"

And then they saw me. I was dead and yet I wasn't dead. My lifeless body slumped forward against the straps of the metal chair in the gas chamber and yet I was standing there watching them.

"Go away! Go away!" the little men screamed, waving their arms frantically. The others were silent, open-mouthed, with fear in their eyes. One of them waved the little men to be silent and stepped forward.

"You're dead," he boomed accusingly, glaring at me.

"I'm dead," I agreed.

Suddenly fear and perplexity turned into resentment. I was seized, returned to Death Row. But it was not the Death

Row the eye of the visitor might see; it was the Death Row the mind of the doomed man knew, a place where hope is mocked.

The ones who had seized me tried to induce me with threats and promises to tell those waiting to die that the only real freedom, for them, was death. But the five dozen executed dead I had known appeared and shook their heads. I refused to utter the lie.

"You'll regret this, you fool! We have ways of dealing with you!"

The night was long. In the morning I was removed in chains from this eerie Death Row of the doomed man's mind. We crossed the prison yard. The sun blazed down. I'd left the darkness behind! We came to a small, guarded, isolated building. Inside was an eight-sided cell, with thick glass windows and two metal chairs.

The gas chamber!

Hands roughly shoved me into the cell. The steel door slammed. A voice boomed out, echoing and reechoing:

"Because of you, fool, this chamber will no longer be used. So we are making you a present of it. This is your reward. This is where you will remain. Forever!" . . .

And then I awoke.

78 *Perhaps the greatest deprivation resulting from spatial confinement is that of free association with other human beings. The casual, affectionate touch or embrace is forbidden or misunderstood; natural fulfillment of sexual passion is not possible. Some inmates, locked up all their adolescent and adult lives, have never had any physical contact with a woman; they do not even know whether or not they are heterosexual. Inside prison, homosexual rape, prostitution, and*

fighting and killing incited by rivalry are common; but there are occasionally more sustaining relationships. This photograph was taken by Robert Neese, an inmate of the Iowa State Prison.

79   *In August 1961, Clarence Earl Gideon was tried for theft in the Circuit Court of Bay County, Florida. He was then fifty-one years old, a drifter, poorly educated; it was his fourth encounter with the law. Because he was destitute he asked the court to appoint a lawyer for him. His request was refused on the grounds that Florida provided free counsel only in cases involving capital crimes. Gideon presented*

his own defense; he was found guilty and sentenced to five years in prison.

But Gideon continued to insist that he had been deprived of his constitutional rights and petitioned the United States Supreme Court to hear his case against the Florida Court. Although his legal reasoning was not entirely accurate, they did so, and in the historic decision of Gideon v. Wainwright *held for the first time that every poor defendant charged with a serious crime has an absolute right to free counsel. This is the "Petition for a Writ of Certiorari" that Gideon wrote out in pencil on prison stationery and sent together with an affidavit* in forma pauperis *to the United States Supreme Court.*

To: The Honorable Earl Warren, Chief Justice of the United States.

Comes now the petitioner, Clarence Earl Gideon, a citizen of the United States of America, in proper person, and appearing as his own counsel. Who petitions this Honorable Court for a Writ of Certiorari directed to the Supreme Court of the State of Florida. To review the order and judgement of the court below denying the petitioner a writ of Habeus Corpus.

Petitioner submits that the Supreme Court of the United States has the authority and jurisdiction to review the final judgement of the Supreme Court of the State of Florida the highest court of the state. Under sec. 344(B) Title 28 U.S.C.A. and because the "Due process clause" of the fourteenth admendment of the constitution and the fifth and the sixth articales of the Bill of rights has been violated. Furthermore, the decision of the court below denying the petitioner a Writ of Habeus Corpus is also inconsistent and adverse to its own previous decisions in paralled cases. . . .

Petitioner contends that he has been deprived of due process of law Habeus Corpus petition alleging that the lower state court has decided a federal question of substance, in a way not in accord with the applicable decisions of this Honorable Court. When at the time of the petitioners trial he ask the lower court for the aid of counsel. The court refused this aid. Petitioner told the court that this court had made decision to the effect that all citizens tried for a felony crime should have aid of counsel. The lower court ignored this plea. . . .

On the 3rd June 1961 A.D. your petitioner was arrested for foresaid crime and convicted for same, Petitioner recieve trial and sentence without aid of counsel, your petitioner was deprived 'Due process of law.'

Petitioner, was deprived of due process of law in the court below. Evidence in the lower court did not show that a crime of Breaking and Entering with the intent to commit Petty Larceny had been committed. Your petitioner was compelled to make his own defense, he was incapable adequately of making his own defense. Petitioner did not plead nol contender But that is what his trial amounted to.

Wherefore the premises considered it is respectfully contented that the decision of the court below was in error and the case should be review by this court, accordingly the writ prepared and prayed for should be issue.

It is respectfully submitted

Clarence Earl Gideon
P.O. Box 221
Raiford Florida

80 *In May 1963 a group of men and women committed to nonviolent action started out on a walk from Quebec to Cuba to protest the United States' military policies. As it passed through the South it also protested discrimination against blacks. Walkers carried signs with such messages as: "Extend Freedom with Nonviolent Action"; "Love Not Hate, Bread Not Bombs"; "End Racial Discrimination"; and they distributed leaflets explaining their views. When the racially integrated group tried to walk through the business district of Albany, Georgia, they were jailed for parading in disobeyance of orders.*

In prison they fasted, an action that they recognized as provocative, but that they hoped would force their captors freely to look at things in a different way. They communicated with each other extensively, seeking and giving support and explaining their individual approaches to nonviolent action. Some noncooperated entirely, some tried water fasting, many broke their fasts while friends in the same cell continued. Finally representatives of the group were allowed to walk the five previously forbidden blocks.

Ray Robinson, Jr., joined the walkers in Philadelphia. At one time he was so filled with rage toward whites that he became a prizefighter so that he could hit one. Then he accepted the profound challenges of nonviolence as a means to radical social change. Robinson was imprisoned for twenty-four days the first time the group was jailed, and, after ten days' release, for twenty-seven days during the second jailing. This letter presents some of the personal tensions involved in radical nonviolent action.

delivered 2/8/64   Albany Co. Jail, Albany, Ga. 3 a.m.
I will not try to write and justify my act of yesterday. I will try to explain it. Yes I pulled up the commode in the City Jail. I pulled this up for attention. I would not have done it if I could have trusted my nonviolence. No, I did not trust my nonviolence. I knew if I did something like this, Chief Pritchett would find a place for me, probably the County Jail. And I was right in my assumptions. I believed if I had stayed in the "Hold" with all of these people (29 in all) I would've become more and more angry. But the main reason is because, I didn't want to see Barbara Deming and Yvonne taken out to go to the hospital. Yes, I want them to get treatment, but I think [Dr.] Hilsman and Pritchett have waited too long with these two. They're playing a game and this game can be very serious, serious enough to be fatal. Some of you will say, "This is all in the commitments of nonviolence." I'll agree but I'm the only one who knows myself. I know I will get charged with destroying city property, and I intend on pleading guilty to the charge. I would rather be charged with this than be charged

with hitting Pritchett or one of his police officers. I would be the one to embarrass this project or no one on it. I know when I've taken about all the harassment I possibly can take, Pritchett has become very hostile toward me. And by his knowing my background, he has started picking on this to provoke me into a fight. I say now, I don't *think* I'll fight back at him, I don't think. But if one of those people dies or ruins their health, I really don't know what I'll do. . . . We have went and been on a food fast, and some have already taken on water fasts, and I believe some will die for their moral convictions. I'm for one who will and I know there's more. . . . But by being over here in the county jail, I'm in a very quiet cell, beside Bradford Lyttle and it's quiet, too. I've never been a man for too much noise and around too many people, especially around some who would like to make me strike them. As I said before, we of the walk and all our supporters have suffered quite a bit here in Albany, the last time I lost about 30 some odd pounds. This time I don't know how much I'll lose. The rest have lost quite a few more. After going through all of this the group and I, I would not be the one to turn to violence and by knowing myself I prefer solitary to make sure. . . . Ray Robinson, Jr.

Yvonne Klein fasted for twenty-five days throughout the first jail term and thirty-five days throughout the second. She suffered from scurvy and such severe malnutrition that prison officials force-fed her, both intravenously and, painfully, by means of a nose tube.

Surprisingly, the fasters found that it eased their discomfort to talk in minute detail about all kinds of food. A wry sense of humor helped, too. These are two of Ms. Klein's notes, composed to cheer and entertain the men in the "hole."

Dear Troglodites—

I have been asleep for some days now, but when I wake up I think about you. For Ralph especially: fresh mushroom soup (not canned, not cream of), Quiche Lorraine, a salad with 3 kinds of lettuce, raspberry ice, elegant cookies. For Marv: a large slice of halvah. For everybody: LOVE, FREEDOM, JOY. If I don't arise again until Feb. 14:   ♡ ♡ ♡ ♡ ♡ Yvonne.

Saturday

Now, as far as meals go, you know we have no cooking committee, so it is inappropriate at this time to address requests to it now. (Or at *any* time—it doesn't exist). However, potato salad is all right, but our taste seems to run more to cream cheese & pecan (& or olive) sandwiches, chocolate ice cream and bananas & fruit juice. Notice—none of this needs cooking —we can gulp it right down—Women are both more radical & more practical. Actually, of course, as we all know, the most radical action is always the most practical. "If the Fool would persist in his Folly, he would become Wise."

81 *Prior to 1967 the Arkansas penitentiary system, consisting of two large farms, was run with one aim only: to earn a profit for the state's general fund. The Cummins Farm, its major facility—16,000 acres and about 1,300 inmates—showed a surplus of over a million dollars in 1966 through the free-market sale of such agricultural commodities as rice, strawberries, and cotton. One of the officers was quoted as saying, "If we work this farm, we need a strap to do it." Flogging was officially permitted and beatings with heavy leather straps, hoe handles, lead-filled rubber hose, and chains were commonplace. The farm operated with a handful of free-world guards and around four hundred inmate trusties, about half of whom were armed guards and had the power of life and death over their charges. Extortion, graft, gambling, and capricious brutality were rife on all levels.*

In 1966 a shocking pattern of torture and venality was uncovered at Tucker Farm, the smaller Arkansas facility, and in 1967 a new

administration set about reforming and reorganizing the entire peni-
tentiary system. Such rehabilitative programs as education and voca-
tional training were established and efforts were made to eliminate
the convict-guard system.

Nevertheless in 1970 a federal court found that confinement in the
isolation cells of the Cummins Farm constituted cruel and unusual
punishment; they were eight-by-ten-foot concrete boxes in which an
average of four, but often as many as eleven, inmates were locked up.
It was also found that the state failed to discharge its duty to protect
inmates from violent assaults, injuries, and death at the hands of
other inmates; they slept in cagelike barracks, fifty to one hundred
percent overcrowded, patrolled only by inmate guards.

This valedictory by the editor Wade Eaves and the cartoons which
follow are from The Pea Pickers Picayune, *the Cummins Farm*
inmate weekly, which was started as part of the 1967 reform move-
ment and was officially uncensored.

How does one say "Goodbye" to Hell?

How do you say goodbye to a nauseous pit of degeneration
. . . a *factory* of heart-corroding fear and distrust; a rendering
plant that can shred strength and ambition into lifelessness?

How do you say goodbye to the mass of inhabitants of this
awesome machine; men who for so long have lived jammed
against your very soul.

How do you say goodbye to a seemingly *taken-for-granted* rag
of a paper called the Pea Pickers' Picayune? It has been a tower
of the greatest strength during the late hours when a man's
mind gropes through the maze of sickening history that brought
him here.

A spare-time insignificant rag, yes, but out of the grimness of
nothingness it kept the hand and the mind busy and perhaps
brought a smile to a man who needed to smile.

A friend said, "Don't get Up-Tight, man . . . get the ———

out of here and forget the joint." A formula, of sorts, and one probably used by a thousand men in the past; quick! easy! fade away . . . leave and kill this steel and concrete memory forever.

IS that the way most men go? Leaving not as a human with dignity but fleeing as an animal flees a forest fire. It would be momentarily easy to leap upon a mental white charger and ride off "in all directions at once" but each idyllic path eventually stops at a barrier of reality.

Fleeing can't erase memories of this place. Running only creates distorted and false memories and transforms them to chaotic images of pseudo-status, of power or symbols of some dreamlike toughness or brotherhood of a life that never should have been. "Escaping" is no solution. The scars are here, laced throughout the mind and body, and they must not ever be forgotten.

How do you say good-bye without some regret? You wonder why you didn't do more to help all the men you *could* have. Like the kid you *knew* was going to escape with the wrong gang . . . he was pathetically simple, easily influenced . . . and he lost his life trying to swim a river. He *could* have been turned away . . . but trying to give good advice isn't the way of the life as accepted here . . . but you should have tried anyway . . . for right is still right.

How many could have been helped . . . dissuaded one time . . . encouraged another . . . so your regret is the shameful knowledge you didn't do all you could to lend a helping hand.

That regret is a gnawing inside, almost a torment, grinding away at you for not being a man when you should. Paradoxically, this knot of regret comes at a time when your soul is a raging inferno of freedom's fire.

There is also a fleeting flash of fear you might have missed seeing or hearing one hideous act or condition or person you could not possibly forget. You can't afford to forget; you can't flee that which is terrifying; you know you mustn't enjoy the luxury of forgetting. You know you *must* keep this Colossus of Shame in proper perspective or fail.

You've been classified a criminal. You have paid for that accusation. You know where the mistakes of life can, and do, lead . . . you've been there.

You've been to Hell.

82 *The trial of the Chicago Eight, who were accused of conspiring to incite a riot, and of succeeding in doing so, when they led demonstrations against the war in Vietnam and other social grievances at the 1968 Democratic Convention* (United States of America, Plaintiff, v. David T. Dellinger et al., Defendants), *has been described as a judicial riot. Established courtroom behavior was abandoned with defense, prosecution, and court each dramatically acting out their partisanship in an extension of the conflict between radical revolutionary forces and the status quo. After five months of testimony, five of the defendants were found guilty of rioting and sentenced to five years and fines of five thousand dollars each. In addition they were ordered to pay the cost of prosecution—nearly a quarter of a million dollars. Although all the defendants were acquitted on the conspiracy charge, both they and their counsel were given sentences for contempt of court ranging from six months to two years.*

During World War II David Dellinger was imprisoned for three years at Danbury, Connecticut, for refusing to enter the draft. There he spent sixty-five days in solitary confinement and fasted in a successful protest against racial segregation in the mess hall. He has continued his vigorous protest of the United States involvement in war.

The following excerpt is from Dellinger's statement to the court, made after conviction but before sentencing for rioting at the 1968 Democratic Convention.

"Been here long?"

"Horthwurt, I'm sick and tired of you fighting me!"

I think that every judge should be required to serve time in prison, to spend time in prison before sentencing other people there, so that he might become aware of the degrading and anti-human conditions that persist not only in Cook County jail but in the prisons generally of this country. . . . I feel that you are a man who has had too much power over the lives of too many people for too many years. You have sentenced them to those degrading conditions that I am talking about without being aware fully of what you are doing, and undoubtedly feeling correct and righteous, as often happens when people do the most abominable things.

I think that in 1970 perhaps the American people will begin to discover something about the nature of the prison system, the system in which we are now confined and which thousands of other political prisoners are confined.

The Black Panthers have said that all Black prisoners are political prisoners, and I think that although it may be hard for people to understand, I think that all people in prison are political prisoners. They are in prison, most of them, because they have violated the property and power concepts of the society; and the bank robber I talked to yesterday was only trying to get his in the ways he thought were open to him, just as businessmen and others profiteer and try to advance their own economic cause at the expense of their fellows. . . .

I want to say that sending us to prison, any punishment the government can impose upon us, will not solve the problems that have gotten us into "trouble" with the government and the law in the first place; will not solve the problem of this country's rampant racism, will not solve the problem of the economic injustice, it will not solve the problem of the foreign policy and the attacks upon the under-developed people of the world. . . .

I think I shall sleep better and happier and with greater sense of fulfillment in whatever jails I am in for the next, however many years, than if I had compromised, if I had pretended the problems were any less real than they are, or if I had sat here passively in the courthouse while justice was being throttled and the truth was being denied.

I learned that when I spent my three years in jail before. When I ended up in the hole and on a hunger strike for sixty-five days, I found out that there are no comforts, no luxuries, no honors, nothing that can compare with having a sense of one's own integrity—not [one's] own infallibility because I have continued to make mistakes from that day to this, but at least one's knowledge is that in his own life, in his own committment, he is living up to the best that he knows. . . .

83   *In November 1970, inmates of Folsom Prison, California, issued a manifesto of demands aimed at bettering prison conditions. It covered medical care, visiting facilities, labor conditions, and wages, the in-prison punitive process, a strong statement on the persecution of politicized prisoners, and a plan for an inmate grievance procedure. The manifesto was a new form of inmate communication and became a model for convict groups seeking a voice in the reform of existing prison structures. Part of its preamble and several of the most important demands follow.*

We the men of Folsom Prison have been committed to the State Correctional Authorities by the people of society for the purpose of correcting what has been deemed as social errors in behavior. Errors which have classified us as socially unacceptable until reprogrammed with new values and more thorough understanding as to our roles and responsibilities as members of the outside community. . . .

The programs which we are submitted to under the facade of rehabilitation, is relative to the ancient stupidity of pouring water on a drowning man, inasmuch as we are treated for our hostilities by our program administrators with their hostility as a medication. In our efforts to comprehend on a feeling level an existence contrary to violence, we are confronted by our captors with violence. In our efforts to comprehend society's code of ethics as to what is fair and just, we are victimized by exploitation and the denial of the celebrated due process of law.

In our peaceful efforts to assemble in dissent as provided under this Nation's United States Constitution, we are in turn murdered, brutalized and framed on various criminal charges because we seek the rights and privileges of ALL AMERICAN PEOPLE.

In our efforts to intellectually expand in keeping with the outside world, through all categories of News Media, we are systematically restricted and punitively offended to isolation status when we insist on our human rights to the wisdom of awareness.

We demand that each man presently held in the Adjustment Center be given a written notice with the Warden of Custody signature on it explaining the exact reason for his placement in the severely restrictive confines of the Adjustment Center.

We demand an end to the segregation of prisoners from the mainline population because of their political beliefs.

We demand the passing of a minimum and maximum term bill which calls for an end to indeterminate sentences whereby a man can be warehoused indefinitely, rehabilitated or not. That all prisoners have the right to be paroled after serving their minimum term instead of the cruel and unusual punishment of being confined beyond his minimum eligibility for parole, and never knowing the reason for the extension of time, nor when his time is completed. . . .

We demand that industries be allowed to enter the Institutions and employ inmates to work eight hours a day and fit into the category of workers for scale wages. The working conditions in prisons do not develop working incentives parallel to the money jobs in the outside society, and a paroled prisoner faces many contradictions on the job that adds to his difficulty to adjust. . . .

We demand that inmates be granted the right to support their own families; at present thousands of welfare recipients have to divide their checks to support their imprisoned relatives who without the outside support could not even buy toilet articles or food. Men working on scale wages could support themselves and families while in prison. . . .

We demand that correctional officers be prosecuted as a matter of law for shooting inmates, around inmates, or any act of cruel and unusual punishment where it is not a matter of life or death. . . .

We demand that all condemned prisoners, avowed revolutionaries and prisoners of war be granted political asylum in the countries under the Free World Revolutionary Pact. . . .

We strongly demand that the State and Prison Authorities conform to recommendation #1 of the "Soledad Caucus Report," to wit,
    "That the State Legislature create a fulltime salaried board of

overseers for the State Prisons. The board would be responsible for evaluating allegations made by inmates, their families, friends, and lawyers against employees charged with acting inhumanely, illegally or unreasonably. The board should include people nominated by a psychological or psychiatric association, by the State Bar Association or by the Public Defenders Association, and by groups of concerned, involving laymen. . . ."

84 *Although his lawyer told him he would get county time—a short sentence—if he pleaded guilty, George Jackson received from one year to life for stealing seventy dollars from a gas station; he was then eighteen years old. Never submitting to the stultifying repressions of prison life, he disciplined his body and honed his mind through rigorous study, especially of such writers as Marx, Lenin, Trotsky, Fanon, and Mao. He dedicated himself to forging a black revolutionary consciousness and became a symbol of resistance to oppression both inside and outside of prison. Jackson was shot and killed at San Quentin on August 21, 1971, allegedly while trying to escape.*

George Jackson spent his entire adult life in prison—eight and a half of those eleven years in solitary confinement; nevertheless he grew in his ability to form strong human relationships. The following letter was written to a childhood friend who, a few weeks previously, had visited him with her mother.

April 11, 1970

Dear Z.,

I received your letter late this afternoon. I've picked it up twenty-five times since then, reading things into it, holding it to my nose, fixing myself on the picture I have of you in my mind.

I am very pleased to have someone so warm, and so soft, and so lovely come into my miserable life; I haven't met *any* selfless, intelligent (mentally liberated), and aggressive women before now, before you. I knew that you existed but I had never had the pleasure. I am uneasy thinking that you may be attracted to the tragedy of me. I hope not, because my response to you is perfectly personal, your eyes, your voice, your walk, hands, mouth. It just occurred to me that I've never noticed any of these things in Frances or Penny or Delora [his sisters]. I like you a lot.

But I am in such a hurry!

My life is so disrupted so precarious, my inclinations so oriented to struggle that anyone who would love me would have to be bold indeed—or out of their head. But if you're saying what I think you are saying I like it. (If I have flattered myself please try to understand.) I like the way you say it also; over the next few months we'll discuss the related problems. By the time I've solved these minor ones that temporarily limit my movements we'll have also settled whether or not it is selfish for us to seek gratification by reaching and touching and holding; does the building of a bed precede the love act itself? Or can we "do it in the road" until the people's army has satisfied our territory problem? That is important to me whether or not you are willing to "do it in the road." You dig, I'm more identifiable with Ernesto than with Fidel. When this is over I immediately go under.

I want to see you! I understand the problems involved, money and transportation, but use your imagination, soldier. Are you getting your social security? That should hold you until you find work. I hate to appear selfish, but you have destroyed my peace here. I have a lot to tell you and some questions.

I'll love you till the wings fly off at least, perhaps beyond. My love could burn you, however, it runs hot and I have nearly half a millennium stored up. Mine is a perfect love, soft to the

touch but so hot, hard, and dense at its center that its weight
will soon offset this planet.

George

85 *The oil painting, opposite, entitled "The Rape of Europa" was done
by Vernell Mitchell, an inmate of the Illinois State Penitentiary at
Statesville.*

86 *Ericka Huggins, an organizer of the Black Panther party in Los
Angeles and in her home state of Connecticut, was imprisoned in
1969 on the double charge of conspiracy to murder and the murder
of New Haven Panther Alex Rackley. She was finally brought to trial
in late 1970 with her accused co-conspirator, Bobby Seale. After
hearing testimony for six months, the jury hung, and in May 1971
the judge dismissed both charges, contending that because of sensational press coverage a fair trial in New Haven was not possible.*

*The following poems were written during her confinement in the
Niantic, Connecticut, prison.*

Sometimes I sit and I think
about you
I forget I am here
—locked away—
I think: Why?
Then, I want to move quickly
silently
and do something. But

I can't and my tears well up
—I am angry at myself
and our comrades for not moving quickly
                                    silently
and reaching out for you.
I can't say: Be strong,
but I can say: know
   that we are with you,
know that we think of you,
know that in our souls
   You are not forgotten.

                              23 October 1970
                              6:15 p.m.

      in limbo—
            to live
               is
         to really raise your
            energy level
               to
            the clouds
            to love
               is
            to really
            exchange energy
               to be here
                  is
            energy-depleting
               exchange . . . impossible.
         soon my level
            will be so low
               i will not know
                  that i
                     am.

One of the emphases of the Black Muslim faith is the regeneration of the fallen through modesty, hard work, and self-discipline, and from the very beginning its members have worked in prisons. However, prison officials and nonbelieving inmates as well have not looked upon the practice of Islam with favor, and its adherents have been harassed. It has taken several court decisions to secure even partial recognition as a legitimate faith, allowing it to hold religious services, to obtain literature, to receive ministers, and to observe its diet. Some of the persecution has been caused by its militant political beliefs, one of its tenets being that the black race will prevail over the white race, which will eventually lose all power. Islam, however, has provided a successful framework for the rehabilitation of many black inmates.

Brother Nelson X, whose testimony appears below, is a prisoner at the Green Haven Correctional Facility in New York State.

In the Name of Allah, Who Came to us in the Person of Master Fard Muhammad. And His Apostle, the Hon. Elijah Muhammad. I greet you, As. Salaam Alaikum.

In this writing I speak not as a spokesman for the Nation of Islam, I speak as a humble follower of Messenger Muhammad. I speak of Islam as a force that gave shape, meaning and direction to my life. I speak of What Islam has done for me. I speak of the greatness I see in Muhammad and the God—Master Fard Muhammad—who sent Elijah, to raise the Black Slave in America. I do not speak in an effort to gain praise, nor do I speak to gain monetary rewards. My reason for speaking is due to my entertainment of the hope that some one who reads it realize that True Leadership lies with the Hon. Elijah Muhammad, Messenger of Allah.

I came in contact with, and embraced Islam in the latter part of 1959. I was in Green Haven Prison, when I heard the Life-giving Soul-stirring teachings of Muhammad. Like most so-called Negroes, I lived a beast's life. I drank anything that would render one void of his senses, I smoked Cancerous Cigarettes, ate poisonous foods, thought poisonous thoughts, Cursed loudly and regularly. I was a deaf, dumb and blind negro in need of Civilization. . . .

I first heard the teachings of Messenger Muhammad from one of his devoted followers. As soon as I heard the teachings, I recognized it as the Truth. I embraced the Truth immediately, and whole-heartedly. I didn't realize I had been looking for the Truth until I found the Truth, and when I found the Truth I realized I had been looking for it. (I pray that you understand.) When I found Muhammad, I found God, I found life, I found Freedom, Justice and Equality. In the Nation of Islam under the guidance of Messenger Muhammad, I have found many do's and don'ts (laws). But when you evaluate these do's and don'ts as I did you learn that each rule or law is designed to render some benefit to the believer. Examples: Don't drink Alcoholic drinks, Don't smoke, Don't eat swine. Be Clean (internally and externally), Don't steal. Surely you will agree with Muhammad —as many wise Doctors agree with him—that Alcoholic drinks, Cigarettes, eating swine, etc. will eventually ruin your Health and steal your life. It is a fool who invited death to his door. Since I don't think of myself as a fool, I ceased drinking, smoking, eating swine. Therefore, I give credit to Muhammad, who found me travelling a path to ill-health and sure death and stopped me—thereby, saving my life. All praise is due to Allah for the Hon. Elijah Muhammad.

I was of those who went the route, regardless. My total faith in God (Allah) and His Messenger, Muhammad, was so great that facing death (which I have faced) would not have turned me away from the Hon. Elijah Muhammad and his teachings. Prison officials and guards underestimated the power of Islam.

Islam—as taught by Messenger Muhammad—enables one to withstand persecution, to withstand pressure, to withstand hunger and discomforts and pains. Islam makes the believer Strong, Fearless and Determined. You can't frighten or intimidate a true follower of Mr. Muhammad. Islam gave me Will-power and great Courage. I always felt that Allah would sustain and protect me—and He did. I bear witness that there is no God but Allah and The Hon. Elijah Muhammad is His Apostle. I have experienced many months in the box and oftentimes there were dangerous moments, but the Divine Guidance I found in Muhammad's Divine Teachings served as a lamp to my feet. . . .

88 *Louis C. Beauchamp, an Assiniboine-Sioux, was born on the Wind River Reservation in Wyoming. When he was three years old the courts took custody of him; he spent twelve years in the Twin Bridges, Montana, Children's Center. Later he was briefly in foster homes, at job corps centers, and in the army, from which he was discharged for going AWOL. For the past few years he has been returned several times to the Montana State Prison at Deer Lodge on burglary convictions. He is currently receiving training under the Manpower Development Act and hopes finally "to make it on the streets." He draws strength from the legends and history of his Indian fathers. Beauchamp calls this poem "Wandering."*

> my soul is wandering
>   for my bones are scattered
> among many museums and
>   private collections of the whiteman.

Sioux Nez Perce Crow Blackfoot
Mohawk . . . .
on & on the names run
        many tribes but all one people
many lost souls adrift
        wailing on lost winds
always hunting

whiteman why?
        for $25.00 perhaps, it's
your greed that
        strikes even beyond death?

at graveside a scream echoes
        on the wind and it tells
of yet another Indian burial site
        robbed and plundered
is nothing sacred anymore

or does your greed excuse that
        explain it so my lost soul
                will know why it wanders.

89 *Tommy Trantino, who in 1963 was convicted of the murder of two
policemen in Lodi, New Jersey, has a strong sense of the absurd; his
rebellion against the prison system and his technique for survival
within it takes a humorous mocking form. In 1969 he put in a request
to the "Chief" for a 5-by-8-foot American flag (without pole) to
display in his cell at all times and a phonograph with a record of Kate
Smith singing "The Star-Spangled Banner" to play before and after
meals. In 1970 he sent his attorney through the regular censored mail
a letter typed on jet black paper. Trantino has said of himself, "I have*

always needed a thick disguise to hide the roles I eat and play."

This is an answer to a form letter from The Center for the Study of Democratic Institutions about his lapsed membership, the salient paragraph of which reads: "Our records also indicate that you have not yet renewed your Center Membership. As you know, your membership in The Center means a great deal to us. If you choose not to continue your membership, it would help us if we knew why."

        dear member is dead
            dear member is
        dead

        broke

        dear member is confined
            dear member is confined in
            the death house of the new
            jersey state prison at trenton dear
        prison   dear member has been
        confined there for the last eight
        for the last eight years
        (so now you know)

        dear member
        is dead
        dear
            member is dead
                broke
        (so ferkyou I now dear
        and now dear you know)
                    yrs,
                    dear member
                    trantino

This is an excerpt from a letter to correspondent "sunlove."

and once a week we fill out our commissary orders and i write
down winston cigarets and instant coffee and stamps and i add
1000 MIRV'S and 25000 tanks and 300000 helicopters and like
that and next week i get my order but they always cross off the
MIRV'S etc. and I don't know why because I know they got all
of that stuff out there and sometimes to show my male
pigginess i write down! raquel welch and 2 kate smith's and
soon and when i get that order slip back i see the boob pig in
charge of robbing us blind out there has written me too and
alison like i was saying you gotta eat yr proteins and dance and i
love to dance and i mean dance dance and i dance like i paint
and i'm a waltzer flowermelter and they used to call me speedo
but my real name was minnie's pearl how deeee

an autobiographical poem

I AM A MAN OF CONVICTION
THEREFORE
I SENTENCE MY SELF TO A LIFETIME OF DEATH
I SENTENCE MYSELF TO A DEATH OF A LIFETIME
I AM A MAN OF CONVICTION
. . . I THINK

90 *John Sinclair was arrested in Detroit in January 1967 for "dispensing
and possessing" two marijuana cigarettes; the dispensing charge was
dropped in June 1969, when the case came to trial, because of the*

police entrapment involved, but he was sentenced for nine and a half to ten years on the possession charge alone. He was confined under maximum security standards in the Jackson, Michigan, prison until December 1971, when he was finally granted an appeal bond.

The following letter was written by Sinclair to the members of the Rainbow People's party, formerly the White Panther party, of which he remained chairman even though imprisoned. It appeared in his column, "Dragon Teeth," in the party's semiweekly, the Ann Arbor Sun.

When we announced in the first issue of the SUN that we had changed the name of our party and had gone through a lot of changes about the kind of work we were doing, we mentioned that we had been discussing this change for a long time before we finally made the decision to name ourselves the Rainbow People's Party. Actually this internal discussion started after Pun and Skip and Jack got captured last July 23rd, because that incident made us aware of some very basic contradictions in the way we were doing things, and it forced us to realize that what we were doing was simply wrong.

The more we investigated our mistakes the clearer it became to us that they all stemmed from the same root—we were trying to deal with things now as if the situation hadn't changed since 1968 when we had first formed the party, and the problem was that things *weren't* the same any more, the whole situation had changed but we hadn't kept up with it, and consequently our activity *couldn't* have the results we hoped it would have. The main problem was that we were still trying to "politicize" freeks and stir them up, whereas they were already stirred up and politicized. . . . People were already ready to move, and what they needed wasn't a lot of slogans and rhetoric but some solid programs and the active assistance of people with experience in doing community self-determination work to guide and help them.

The other main thing was that we had always had the idea that "the revolution" was going to happen spontaneously and at once, like tomorrow or the day after. . . . And in line with this, like I said, we saw our job as being like cheerleaders, going around and stirring people up so they would run out into the streets and "join the revolution" as soon as the apocalypse jumped off. We kept shouting "Off the Pigs" and "All Power to the People" and "Free All Political Prisoners" as if it was enough to spout some slogans and feel real mean and pretty soon the powerstructure would collapse in fear of us. . . .

To make it even worse, we were doing this on a national basis instead of digging in where we were and working with people in our own community. We spent most of our time trying to get "chapters" going all over the country. . . .

So we started trying to cut to the root of our problems and started with the name, the way our "organization" was set up, and the way we lived together with each other in our commune. (I say "we," but Pun and I, who took part in this discussion all the way through, have been imprisoned throughout, and have been able to share in our communal life only through letters and visits.) Some people didn't agree with what we were doing and split, other people had to be asked to leave, some new people came in—but more than that we started reorganizing our most basic methods of thinking and methods of work, starting with the housework, cooking, baby care, the economic work that pays the rent and buys the groceries, the decision-making process, and the way we try to relate to our own people. We decided to suspend publication of the national newspaper until we're ready to do organizing work on a national level, and we made up our mind to get this paper together for the people in the immediate community so we could help get people together and keep them together. . . .

We know we won't get all the people together all at once, but we can start by getting ourselves together right here where we are and moving together to unite with as many people as we can, step by step, building as we go and defending what we

have built, until we start to see our vision of the Rainbow
Nation, the nation to end all nations, come to life. Because that
vision is the most powerful thing we have—it's kept me alive
here in the penitentiary for almost two years, it keeps Pun and
Skip alive, it keeps all of us alive even though we are constantly
surrounded by the biggest death machine in human history. And
more life is what all of us need—LIFE TO THE LIFE
CULTURE! RAINBOW POWER TO THE PEOPLE OF
THE FUTURE! LET IT GROW! LET IT GROW!!

> John Sinclair
> Chairman, Rainbow People's Party
> Jackson Prison, May 4, 1971

In Memoriam: Allison Krause, Jeff Miller, Sandra Lee Scheuer,
Bill Schroeder

91 *This poem, "Fragment," is by Donald Rex Lane, an Indian who was
incarcerated in the Folsom, California, prison at the time he wrote
it.*

> I rebelled
>   I drowned myself in fantasy
> To escape your inert living.
> And now I gasp for breath
>   because I have lingered too long
> Away from reality.

92 *Rioting is an extreme form of communication. On September 9,
1971, the inmates of the Attica (N. Y.) Correctional Facility took over
the prison by force and, using forty-two officer and civilian hostages
as protection, held it for four days. Although the uprising was spon-*

taneous, set off by the rumor that two inmates had been punitively beaten for insolence to a guard, it came at the end of a summer of increasing tension between the proportionately large black, ghetto-raised, and socially aware inmate population and their white, rural custodians. Promised reforms were seen as a threat to discipline by most correction officers and as slow to materialize or a mockery by many inmates.

In a departure from accepted practice, the administration endeavored to retake the facility by negotiation. This proved impossible. On September 13, 1971, the National Guard saturated the inmate stronghold with CS and CN gas and state troopers stormed it with rifles and shotguns. Ten hostages and twenty-nine inmates were killed and over eighty others were seriously wounded by gunfire in the retaking of the prison; with the exception of the Indian massacres, it was the bloodiest one-day encounter between Americans since the Civil War. One hostage and three inmates were killed by the insurgents while they held the prison. Reprisals taken upon the inmates by correction officers after they had been subdued have been described as a second riot.

Because reports of what actually happened at Attica conflicted, the New York State Commission on Attica was appointed in November 1971 to conduct a full and impartial investigation into the facts and circumstances leading up to, during, and following the uprising. As part of its extensive work, it held public televised hearings in April and May 1972 at which a cross-section of eyewitnesses testified. Edward Young was one of the inmate witnesses. Sentenced for from thirty to sixty years in 1960 for second degree murder, Young was questioned by the commission about why, with years of clean record behind him, he was suddenly reprimanded in March 1971 for disobeying an order while marching. His answer has much to say about the relationship of correction officers and inmates and can perhaps be epitomized by these few words: "They expect us to be every day the same."

I eat every day with the guys I work with . . . And I eat on a line where I am the only black man that eats on that side of the line. On this side, they don't separate us. That's something you do to yourself. Nobody makes you eat like that.

So I am in line five minutes to 12:00 getting ready to go to the mess hall. A new officer says, . . . "Get over there with the rest of them." My nose is open. . . . (I)n the other line opposite me, there was fifteen or sixteen blacks and they heard him. And they started, just like that they started.

I said, "Listen, I've eaten over here with these men for two years. I am going to eat there today and tomorrow." I said, "I'm not going to move and you ain't going to move me." And he said, "Let's forget about it. You can do just what you please about it."

I went to the mess hall, came back and was keeplocked.

Question: What do you think would have happened if this officer had told one of the younger inmates that he couldn't stand in line with white inmates?

I don't know. Depends on the individual. Depends on how he was that day. If he had got a letter from home the night before saying his wife had been pregnant and he would have been in jail three years, I don't know what he would have did. These things happen every day. These happen to us. We know what happens.

They expect us to be every day the same. I seen a guy, his mother died in Mississippi. You can't go out of state. And he was the only kid in the family. . . . The next morning this man [officer] lined [the men] up—the first thing he did was hit the stick, line up, get in pairs, be quiet. That's the first thing you hear when you get out of the cell. The officer don't know this guy. He don't feel like getting lined up. He is bugged up to start with. Not at the officer. Just in general, you understand what I mean?

The guys says, "Man, go to hell. I don't feel like it." And that's just what he felt like. Boom, he was locked up. You thought he killed somebody.

93 *On the first day of the rebellion, while much of the prison was still smoldering from fires set by inmates, Attica's disbelieving superintendent asked, "Why are they destroying their homes?" To many inmates the improvised tents in which they sheltered during the four days of the uprising were more of a home than their six-by-nine-by-seven-foot cells ever could be. This photograph was taken after D yard had been cleared; the surviving prisoners had surrendered and were rehoused behind bars.*

V

In the 1970s the major locus of prison reform has been the courts. Significant extensions of the constitutional rights granted to prisoners have taken place as a result of lawsuits by prisoners against rules governing internal prison discipline, especially those concerned with the practice of religion, access to published matter, and correspondence. In April 1972, federal Judge James E. Doyle of the Western District of Wisconsin was asked to decide if administrators of the Wisconsin State Prison could constitutionally prevent an inmate from sending mail to his sister-in-law. Judge Doyle concluded that they could not; for although he was mindful that judicial response to prisoners' rights lawsuits might ultimately cause the disintegration of the institution of prison, he remained convinced that persons convicted of a crime should continue to share with the general population the full latent protection of the First and Fourteenth Amendments. He reasoned that the rules established to regulate prison life were not designed to serve the accepted goals of deterrence or rehabilitation, but rather to insure institutional survival. In a lengthy and innovative opinion, Judge Doyle examined some of the profound issues raised by prisoners' challenges of the rules and regulations to which they are subjected.

"No doubt it will be contended that the central objective of prison is the protection of members of the general population from loss and injury caused by antisocial behavior. Surely this is a governmental objective which is wholly permissible under the Constitution. The problems arise from the choice of prison as a means to achieve it. . . .

"Lawsuits challenging these rules for institutional survival raise peculiarly poignant issues. The genuineness of the prisoners' grievances, the humiliating and degrading effects of many of the rules, the invasion of the innermost core of human privacy, all compel serious and sympathetic attention to these complaints. The genuineness of the concern of the guards and administrators for their own safety and for the protection of some prisoners from other prisoners, the budgetary frustration experienced by correctional officials keenly aware that many of these rules for institutional survival undercut major objectives of their programs, the obvious proposition that the correctional officials are better qualified than the courts to evaluate the necessity for these rules for institutional survival, all compel serious and sympathetic attention to the answers to these complaints.

"In my view, in passing upon these challenges to the rules for institutional survival, the balance must be struck in favor of the individual rights of the prisoners. That is to say, if one of these rules of institutional survival affects significantly a liberty which is clearly protected among the general population, and if its only justification is that the prison cannot survive without it, then it may well be that the Constitution requires that the prison be modified. Specifically, if the functions of deterrence and rehabilitation cannot be performed in a prison without the imposition of a restrictive regime not reasonably related to those functions, it may well be that those functions can no longer be performed constitutionally in a prison setting. Also, with respect to the comparatively few offenders who simply must be physically restrained for periods of time to prevent them from committing antisocial acts, it may well be that the society will be compelled, constitutionally, to allocate sufficient resources for physical facilities and manpower to permit this function of physical restraint to be performed in a setting which little resembles today's prisons. . . .

"I conclude that freedom to use the mails is a First Amendment freedom. . . . I conclude that in the general population, each individual's interest in corresponding by mail with another is fairly to be characterized as a "fundamental" interest. I conclude that when the government undertakes to deny this freedom to a member of the class of persons who have been convicted of crime, while granting it to members of a class of persons who have not been convicted of a crime, the burden is upon the defendant to show a compelling governmental interest in this differential in treatment. . . .

"I find that in denying the plaintiff the opportunity to correspond with his sister-in-law by mail, the defendant and his agents are acting under color of state law, and that they are depriving him, and threaten to continue to deprive him of a right secured to him by the First and Fourteenth Amendments to the Constitution of the United States."

SOURCES

I.   The Philadelphia Society for the Relief of Distressed Prisoners.
      Preamble to rules, 1776. *Pennsylvania Evening Post,* Saturday,
      February 24, 1776, p. 96. Quoted in *Prison Journal,* Vol. XXIV,
      no. 4, Oct. 1944, "The Philadelphia Society for the Relief of
      Distressed Prisoners, 1776–1777" by Negley K. Teeters, pp.
      456–457.

1.   Jonathan Gillet. Letter to his family, 1776. Henry R. Stiles, *Letters
      from the Prisons and Prison-Ships of the Revolution,* New York,
      1865, pp. 7–12.

2.   Prison-ship prisoner. Letter, 1781. Stiles, *op. cit.,* pp. 31–32.

3.   British officers prisoners of war, 1782. Memorial to General Nathanael
      Greene. William L. Clements Library, The University of
      Michigan.

4.   Simeon Baxter. Sermon, 1781. Simeon Baxter, *Tyrannicide proved
      Lawful from the Practice and Writing of Jews Heathens and
      Christians. . . . ,* London, 1782, pp. 30–31.

5.   Abel Davis. Letter to the General Assembly [of Connecticut], 1783.
      Richard H. Phelps, *A History of Newgate of Connecticut,* Albany,
      1860, p. 45.

6.   Norris Jones. Diary entry, 1787. Norris Jones, *Diary whilst in
      Philadelphia Prison.* The Historical Society of Pennsylvania,
      Manuscript Collection.

7.   Francis Uss. Autobiography and confession, 1789. Francis Uss, *The
      Narrative of the Life of Francis Uss. . . . ,* Poughkeepsie, 1789.

8.   Abraham Johnstone. Execution speech, 1797. Abraham Johnstone, *The
      Address of Abraham Johnstone, a Black Man . . . to the People of
      Colour,* Philadelphia, 1797.

9.   Benjamin Bailey. Letter to his wife, 1798. Benjamin Bailey, *The
      Confession of Benjamin Bailey,* Reading, Pa., 1798, pp. 15–16.

10.   John Wright. Letter, 1795. William L. Clements Library, The
      University of Michigan.

11.   New York Debtors' Prison. Minutes and notes, 1795–97. Courtesy The

New-York Historical Society, New York City, Manuscript Collection, William Duer papers.

12. Robert Morris. Letters to J. W. Nicholson, Esq., 1798, and Thomas Stritch, Esq., 1800. The Historical Society of Pennsylvania, Manuscript Collection.

13. Newark, New Jersey, debtor. Letter to the editor of *The Forlorn Hope*, 1800. *The Forlorn Hope*, March 24, 1800.

14. Philip Williams. Letter to John Parrish, 1806. The Historical Society of Pennsylvania, Manuscript Collection, Cox-Parrish-Wharton papers.

15. John Van Horn. Letter to Roberts Vaux, 1818; note of Roberts Vaux. The Historical Society of Pennsylvania, Manuscript Collection, Roberts Vaux papers.

16. Elam Lynds. Letter to the Honorable G. C. Verplanck, 1823. Courtesy The New-York Historical Society, New York City, Manuscript Collection.

17. Nathan Atherton. Letter, 1824. The Historical Society of Pennsylvania, Manuscript Collection, Joseph Watson papers.

18. Ann Price. Letter to Mr. Morgan, 1825. The Historical Society of Pennsylvania, Manuscript Collection, Joseph Watson papers.

19. Charles Mitchell. Letter to Joseph Watson, 1825; Aaron Howell, letter to Joseph Watson, 1825. The Historical Society of Pennsylvania, Manuscript Collection, Joseph Watson papers.

II. Prison Discipline Society, Boston. Ideals, 1826. *First Annual Report of the Board of the Managers of the Prison Discipline Society, Boston, June 2, 1826*, pp. 36–37.

20. Robert Bush. Last words, 1828. *The Trial of Robert Bush*, Springfield, Mass., 1828, p. 15.

21. Nat Turner. Confession, 1831. *The Confessions of Nat Turner, the leader of the late insurrection in Southampton, Va. . . . .* Baltimore, 1831.

22. Gustave de Beaumont and Alexis de Tocqueville. Interviews, 1832. G.A. de Beaumont and A. de Tocqueville, *On the Penitentiary System in the United States, and its Application in France. . . . ,* Philadelphia, 1833, pp. 187–198.

23. Inmate of Auburn Prison, N.Y. Coverlet, 1838. The Long Island Historical Society.

24. Thomas L. Nichols. Letter to Rosalie, 1839. Thomas L. Nichols, *Journal in Jail*, Buffalo, 1840, pp. 98–99.
25. Joseph Smith, Jr. Letter to the Church of Latter-Day Saints at Quincy, Illinois, and Scattered Abroad, and to Bishop Partridge in Particular, 1839. *History of the Church of Jesus Christ of the Latter-Day Saints. Period I. History of Joseph Smith, the Prophet by Himself,* Vol. III. Deseret News, Salt Lake City, Utah, 1905, pp. 302–303.
26. Archilla Smith. Speech after sentencing, 1840; execution speech, 1841. John Howard Payne, *Indian Justice*, Grant Foreman, Ed., Oklahoma City, 1934, pp. 87–88, 102. Originally published in *The New York Journal of Commerce*, April 17, 29, 1841.
27. George Thompson. Exhortation-graffito, 1841. George Thompson, *Prison Life and Reflections*, Oberlin, 1847, pp. 76–77.
28. A. Judson. Suicide note—graffito, c. 1843. Prison Association of New York, *First Annual Report*, New York 1844, p. 25.
29. Women inmates, Ohio Penitentiary. Letter to husband, 1846; letter to mother, 1846. James B. Finley, *Memorials of Prison Life*, Cincinnati, 1853, pp. 105–106, 188–189.
30. Mortimer C. Belden. Song, 1845. *The Albany Freeholder*, July 9, 1845.
31. William and James M. Bradley. Thanksgiving song, 1846. Charles Spear, ed., *Voices from Prison*, Boston, 1848, pp. 213–218.
32. James A. Clay. Book excerpt; letter, 1853. James A. Clay, *A Voice from Prison; or Truths for the Multitude and Pearls for the Truthful*, Boston, 1856, pp. 47, 56, 325.
33. A. C. N. Letter to J. Price, Esq. Sheriff, c. 1850. James Holbrook, *Ten Years among the Mailbags*, Boston, 1856, pp. 233–234.
34. Gerald Toole. Autobiography, 1862. Gerald Toole, *The Life of Gerald Toole*, Hartford, Conn., 1862, pp. 19–20, 24–25, 30–31.
35. William C. Harris. Book excerpt, 1862. William C. Harris, *Prison-Life in the Tobacco Warehouse at Richmond*, Philadelphia, 1862, pp. 62–63.
36. Simeon Bolivar Hulbert. Diary entry, 1862. Courtesy The New-York Historical Society, New York City, Manuscript Collection.
37. Howard C. Wright. Letters to his mother, 1861, 1865; letters to Henry A. Patterson, 1863; letter to his sister Eleanor, 1863. Courtesy The New-York Historical Society, New York City, Manuscript Collection.

38. Andersonville prisoner. Woodcarving, 1864. From the collection of
Norm Flaydermans, New Milford, Conn.

39. Catherine Virginia Baxley. Letter to William H. Seward, Secretary of
State, 1862; diary entries, 1865. U.S. War Dept., *The War of the
Rebellion, Official Records*. Series II. Vol. 2; Manuscript Division,
The New York Public Library, Astor, Lenox and Tilden
Foundation.

40. Henry Wirz. Diary entry, 1865. James L. Williamson, *Prison Life in
the Old Capitol*, West Orange, N.J., 1911, pp. 147–148.

41. Addie Irving. Letters to Mrs. E. C. Buchanan, 1866. Prison Association
of New York Annual Report, 1845. Letters, Courtesy The
New-York Historical Society, New York City, Manuscript
Collection.

42. James Brady. Letter to his daughter, c. 1868; L. Musgrove, letters to
his brother and his wife, 1868; L. P. Griswold, letter to his
common-law wife; conundrum, c. 1869. Thomas L. Dimsdale, *The
Vigilantes of Montana or Popular Justice in the Rocky Mountains*,
Montana Territory, 1866, p. 181. John W. Cook, *Hands Up; or
35 Years of Detective Life in the Mountains and on the Plains*,
Denver, 1897, pp. 117, 229–231.

III. Major A. T. Goshorn. Welcoming address to the National Congress on
Penitentiary and Reformatory Discipline, 1870. The National
Congress on Penitentiary and Reformatory Discipline, Cincinnati,
1870, *Transactions*, Albany, 1871, pp. 1–2.

43. Henry C. Paul. Letter to Judge John Cadwalader, 1871. The Historical
Society of Pennsylvania, Manuscript Collection, Cadwalader
papers.

44. Hamlin. Note to Seth Wilbur Payne, 1873. Seth Wilbur Payne, *Behind
the Bars*, New York, 1873, pp. 1, 29.

45. Bears Heart. Autobiographical speech, 1880; drawing, 1876. Karen
Daniels Peterson, *Plains Indian Art from Fort Marion*, Norman,
Oklahoma, 1971, pp. 99–100. Photograph Courtesy the Museum
of the American Indian, Heye Foundation.

46. William Marcy "Boss" Tweed. Letter to Charles O'Connor, 1876.
Courtesy The New York Historical Society, New York City,
Manuscript Collection. Also in *"Boss" Tweed* by Denis Tilden
Lynch, New York: Boni and Liveright, 1927, pp. 403–404.

47. E. C. Wines. Book excerpt, 1880; North Carolina convict railroad laborers, c. 1880. E. C. Wines, *The State of Prisons and of Child-Saving Institutions in the Civilized World*, 1880, Cambridge, Mass., 1880, p. 202.

48. Cole Younger. Letters to J. W. Buel, 1880. James W. Buel, *The Border Outlaws*, St. Louis, 1881, pp. 228–234.

49. Pedro Dominicus. Horsehair bridle and cinch, 1879. Nebraska State Historical Society.

50. John Purves. Prison reports, c. 1885. *The Menard Time*, Menard, Ill., June 1, 1972, p. 5, August 1, 1972, p. 4. (Reprinted from *The Spectator*, Southern Michigan Prison.)

51. Alexander Berkman. Letter to K., 1896. Alexander Berkman, *Prison Memoirs of an Anarchist*, New York, 1912, pp. 328–329.

52. Geronimo. Autobiography, 1905. S. M. Barrett, ed. *Geronimo, His Own Story*, New York: Ballantine Books, 1970.

53. James Gordon Stell. Poems, 1908. James Stell and John Null, *Convict Verse*, Fort Madison, Ia., 1908, p. 29. Fred High, ed., *Prison Problems*, Chicago, 1913, pp. 116–117.

54. Mamie Slater. Rag dolls, c. 1905. Chester County Historical Society.

55. Arturo Giovannitti. Poem, 1912. Arturo Giovannitti, *Arrows in the Gale*, Riverside, Conn., 1914, pp. 21–27.

56. Anonymous. Poems—graffiti, c. 1910. Walter Wilson, *Hell in Nebraska*, Lincoln, 1913., pp. 11, 41, 94.

57. Steven Nemeth. Essay, 1915. The Mutual Welfare League, Ossining, N.Y. 1916, pp. 2–3.

58. Joseph Hillstrom (Joe Hill). Letter to the editor of *Solidarity*, 1914. *Solidarity*, December 19, 1914.

59. Jesse Harding Pomeroy. Mathematical puzzles, 1916. Jesse Harding Pomeroy, *Selections from the Writings of Jesse Harding Pomeroy, Life Prisoner since 1874*, Boston, 1920, p. 19.

60. Rose Winslow. Notes, 1917. *The Suffragist*, December 1, 1917, p. 5.

61. Ernest L. Meyer. Letter to his wife, 1918. Ernest L. Meyer, *Hey! Yellowbacks!*, New York, 1930, pp. 89–90.

62. Eugene V. Debs. Letter to Warden J. Z. Terrell, 1919. David Fulton Krasner papers. Manuscripts and Archives Division, The New York Public Library. Astor, Lenox and Tilden Foundations.

63. Kate Richards O'Hare. Letters to her family, 1919. *Kate O'Hare's Prison Letters*, Girard, Kansas, 1919, pp. 35, 69–71, 73.

64. Huddie Ledbetter. Song, 1923. Collected and adapted by John A. Lomax and Allan Lomax, Folkways Music Publishers, Inc., New York.

65. Charles Chapin. Letter to the editor of *House and Garden*, 1922; aviary and garden, 1922–1929. *House and Garden*, February, 1922. Photograph. State of New York, Department of Correctional Services.

66. Bartolomeo Vanzetti. Letter to Mrs. Maude Pettyjohn, 1925. Marion Denman Frankfurter and Gardner Jackson, eds., *The Letters of Sacco and Vanzetti*, New York: Viking, 1928, pp. 144–145.

67. Nicola Sacco. Letter to Mrs. Cerise Jack, 1926. Frankfurter, *op. cit.*, pp. 35–6.

68. Samuel Roth. Book excerpt, 1928. Samuel Roth, *Stone Walls Do Not. . . . The Chronicle of a Captivity*, New York, 1930, pp. 52, 141–142.

69. Robert Joyce Tasker. Editorial, 1929. *The Bulletin*, San Quentin, Calif., July 1929.

IV. Prison Association of New York. Appraisal of reform opportunities, 1930. *86th Annual Report*, New York, 1931, p. 20.

70. Victor F. Nelson. Book excerpt, 1931. Victor F. Nelson, *Prison Days and Nights*, Boston: Little, Brown and Co., 1933, pp. 14–16.

71. King Kong. Song, c. 1930. Paul Warren, *Next Time is for Life*, New York: Dell, 1953, p. 71.

72. Dannemora, N.Y., inmate. Letter to Margaret Sanger, 1940. The Sophia Smith Collection, Smith College, Northampton, Mass., Margaret Sanger papers.

73. Japanese internees. Newspaper articles, 1942. *Santa Anita Pacemaker*, Santa Anita Assembly Center, July 25, 1942.

74. Atlanta Federal Penitentiary inmates. War work, 1944. *The Atlantian*, May-June 1944, p. 3.

75. Alger Hiss. Letters to his wife and son, 1952. Meyer L. Zeligs, *Friendship and Fratricide*, New York: Viking, 1967. Final paragraph of second letter from unpublished material.

76. Thomas Licavoli. Autobiographical essay, 1952; Ohio Penitentiary inmate, First-day cover, 1971.

77. Caryl Chessman. Book excerpt, 1954. Caryl Chessman, *Trial by Ordeal*, Englewood Cliffs, N.J.: Prentice-Hall, Inc., 1955, pp. 290–293.

78. Robert Neese. Photograph, 1958. Robert Neese, *Prison Exposures*, Philadelphia, 1959, p. 52.

79. Clarence Earl Gideon. Petition for a Writ of Certiorari, 1961. *Gideon v. Wainwright*, 155 Oct. Term 1962 U.S. Supreme Court. (Originally *Gideon v. Cochran*, No. 890 Misc. Oct. Term 1961, U.S. Supreme Court.)

80. Ray Robinson, Jr. Letter to fellow inmates, 1964; Yvonne Klein, notes to fellow inmates, 1964. Barbara Deming, *Prison Notes*, New York: Grossman, 1966.

81. Wade Eaves. Editorial, 1969; cartoons, 1968. Cummins Farm, Arkansas Penitentiary, *The Pea Pickers Picayune*, August 31, September 14, 1968; May 2, 1969.

82. David T. Dellinger. Pre-sentencing statement to the court, 1970. *United States of America v. David T. Dellinger, et al.* No. 69 CR 180, U.S. District Court, Northern District of Illinois, verbatim transcript, pp. 21952–4, 21956–7, 21962–3.

83. Inmates of Folsom Prison, California. Manifesto, 1970. Mimeographed copy.

84. George Jackson. Letter to Z., 1970. George Jackson, *Soledad Brother, The Prison Letters of George Jackson*, New York: Bantam Books, 1970, pp. 208–209.

85. Vernell Mitchell. Painting, 1970. Collection of Herbert Hemphill, New York.

86. Ericka Huggins. Poems, 1970.

87. Nelson X. Canady. Witness of faith, 1972. Letter to C. O. Philip.

88. Louis C. Beauchamp. Poem, 1972. *The Hunter*, Deer Lodge, Montana. March-April, 1972, p. 25.

89. Thomas Trantino. Letter-poem, 1970; letter to sunlove, 1971; poem, 1972.

90. John Sinclair. Newspaper column, 1971. *Ann Arbor Sun* (published by the Rainbow People's Party), May 14–20, 1971, p. 4.

91. Donald Rex Lane. Poem, 1971. *Akwesasne Notes*, Late Autumn, 1971.

92.   Edward Young. Testimony, 1972. New York State Special Commission
        on Attica, verbatim transcript of public hearings, April 14, 1972,
        pp. 618–621.
93.   Inmate of Attica Correctional Facility, New York. Shelter in D yard,
        1971. New York State Police photograph released by the New
        York State Special Commission on Attica.

V.   District Judge James E. Doyle. Opinion, 1972. *Juan G. Morales v.
        Wilbur J. Schmidt*, 340 F. Supp. 544 (W.D. Wis. 1972).

73 74 10 9 8 7 6 5 4 3 2 1

In this compelling anthology Cynthia
Owen Philip has brought together a
unique collection of prison communications which cover the history of this country from the Revolutionary War to Attica.
They are as different as the people who
wrote them.

While IMPRISONED IN AMERICA
focuses on the common criminal, also included are works by prisoners who are not
usually considered in the traditional role:
suffragists, war demonstrators, American
Indians, and Japanese internees. Through
its unusual historical presentation we are
brought to a fuller awareness that prisoners, although we have continually tried
to keep them out of our waking consciousness, are indeed an integral part and expression of our way of life.

This anthology includes prison artwork,
songs, handicrafts as well as graffiti, diary
excerpts and letters, for writing is not the
only form of communication for prisoners,
just as it is not the only channel for men
in the free world.

The selections are not lacking in humor,
tenderness, irony, or grace, for it is "this
reaching out of an individual, this risking